How China Opened Its Door

Integrating National Economies: Promise and Pitfalls

Barry Bosworth (Brookings Institution) and Gur Ofer (Hebrew University)
Reforming Planned Economies in an Integrating World Economy

Ralph C. Bryant (Brookings Institution)
International Coordination of National Stabilization Policies

Susan M. Collins (Brookings Institution/Georgetown University)
Distributive Issues: A Constraint on Global Integration

Richard N. Cooper (Harvard University)
Environment and Resource Policies for the World Economy

Ronald G. Ehrenberg (Cornell University)
Labor Markets and Integrating National Economies

Barry Eichengreen (University of California, Berkeley)
International Monetary Arrangements for the 21st Century

Mitsuhiro Fukao (Bank of Japan)
Financial Integration, Corporate Governance, and the Performance of Multinational Companies

Stephan Haggard (University of California, San Diego)
Developing Nations and the Politics of Global Integration

Richard J. Herring (University of Pennsylvania) and Robert E. Litan (Department of Justice/Brookings Institution)
Financial Regulation in the Global Economy

Miles Kahler (University of California, San Diego)
International Institutions and the Political Economy of Integration

Anne O. Krueger (Stanford University)
Trade Policies and Developing Nations

Robert Z. Lawrence (Harvard University)
Regionalism, Multilateralism, and Deeper Integration

Sylvia Ostry (University of Toronto) and Richard R. Nelson (Columbia University)
Techno-Nationalism and Techno-Globalism: Conflict and Cooperation

Robert L. Paarlberg (Wellesley College/Harvard University)
Leadership Abroad Begins at Home: U.S. Foreign Economic Policy after the Cold War

Peter Rutland (Wesleyan University)
Russia, Eurasia, and the Global Economy

F. M. Scherer (Harvard University)
Competition Policies for an Integrated World Economy

Susan L. Shirk (University of California, San Diego)
How China Opened Its Door: The Political Success of the PRC's Foreign Trade and Investment Reforms

Alan O. Sykes (University of Chicago)
Product Standards for Internationally Integrated Goods Markets

Akihiko Tanaka (Institute of Oriental Culture, University of Tokyo)
The Politics of Deeper Integration: National Attitudes and Policies in Japan

Vito Tanzi (International Monetary Fund)
Taxation in an Integrating World

William Wallace (St. Antony's College, Oxford University)
Regional Integration: The West European Experience

Susan L. Shirk

How China Opened Its Door

The Political Success of the
PRC's Foreign Trade and
Investment Reforms

THE BROOKINGS INSTITUTION
Washington, D.C.

Copyright © 1994
THE BROOKINGS INSTITUTION
1775 Massachusetts Avenue, N. W., Washington, D.C. 20036

Library of Congress Cataloging-in-Publication data:
Susan L. Shirk
How China opened its door: The political success of the PRC's foreign
trade and investment reforms/Susan L. Shirk
p. cm. — (Integrating national economies)
Includes bibliographical references and index.
ISBN 0-8157-7854-6 (cloth: alk. paper) — ISBN 0-8157-7853-8
(pbk: alk. paper)
1. China—Commercial policy. 2. China—Economic policy—1976–
I. Title. II. Series: Integrating national economies.
HF1604.S57 1994   94-26558
338.951—dc20   CIP

9 8 7 6 5 4 3 2 1

The paper used in this publication meets the minimum requirements of
American National Standard for Information Sciences—Permanence of Paper
for Printed Library Materials, ANSI Z39.48-1984

Typeset in Plantin

Composition by Princeton Editorial Associates
Princeton, New Jersey

Printed by R. R. Donnelley and Sons Co.
Harrisonburg, Virginia

The Brookings Institution is an independent organization devoted to nonpartisan research, education, and publication in economics, government, foreign policy, and the social sciences generally. Its principal purposes are to aid in the development of sound public policies and to promote public understanding of issues of national importance.

The Institution was founded on December 8, 1927, to merge the activities of the Institute for Government Research, founded in 1916, the Institute of Economics, founded in 1922, and the Robert Brookings Graduate School of Economics and Government, founded in 1924.

The Board of Trustees is responsible for the general administration of the Institution, while the immediate direction of the policies, program, and staff is vested in the President, assisted by an advisory committee of the officers and staff. The by-laws of the Institution state: "It is the function of the Trustees to make possible the conduct of scientific research, and publication, under the most favorable conditions, and to safeguard the independence of the research staff in the pursuit of their studies and in the publication of the results of such studies. It is not a part of their function to determine, control, or influence the conduct of particular investigations or the conclusions reached."

The President bears final responsibility for the decision to publish a manuscript as a Brookings book. In reaching his judgment on the competence, accuracy, and objectivity of each study, the President is advised by the director of the appropriate research program and weighs the views of a panel of expert outside readers who report to him in confidence on the quality of the work. Publication of a work signifies that it is deemed a competent treatment worthy of public consideration but does not imply endorsement of conclusions or recommendations.

The Institution maintains its position of neutrality on issues of public policy in order to safeguard the intellectual freedom of the staff. Hence interpretations or conclusions in Brookings publications should be understood to be solely those of the authors and should not be attributed to the Institution, to its trustees, officers, or other staff members, or to the organizations that support its research.

Foreword

FOREIGN trade and investment reforms have transformed the
People's Republic of China from a closed economy to a major
trading power. China has become the world's tenth largest exporter
and the largest recipient of foreign direct investment in the developing
world. In this book, Susan Shirk tells the story of how China ended its
long-held policies of economic isolationism and rejoined the world
economy during the decade and a half between 1979 and 1994.

In addressing the question of how such a turnaround was accomplished, the author looks for answers in politics instead of economics.
She describes how China's political institutions have shaped economic policymaking and produced reforms characterized by gradualism, administrative decentralization, and particularism. The author
examines several of the most important foreign economic reforms:
the establishment of special regional zones, decentralization of trade
management, reform of the foreign exchange regime, and opening of
the domestic market. The book concludes by considering the international pressures for and domestic political obstacles to China's
deep integration with the world economy, which would involve adoption of international standards for intellectual property, environmental protection, and the treatment of labor.

Susan L. Shirk is the director of the University of California's
systemwide Institute on Global Conflict and Cooperation and a
professor in the Graduate School of International Relations and
Pacific Studies and the Department of Political Science at the University of California, San Diego. She is grateful to Nicholas Lardy for his
extensive suggestions about the manuscript, Tim Fitzpatrick for re-

search assistance, and the participants in a Brookings review conference and the series editors for helpful feedback. She also wishes to thank Nancy Davidson, who edited the manuscript; Laura Kelly, who verified its factual content; and Trudy Elkins, who provided administrative support. Lisa L. Guillory provided word processing assistance, and Princeton Editorial Associates prepared the index.

Funding for the project came from the Center for Global Partnership of the Japan Foundation, the Curry Foundation, the Ford Foundation, the Korea Foundation, the Tokyo Club Foundation for Global Studies, the United States-Japan Foundation, and the Alex C. Walker Educational and Charitable Foundation. The authors and Brookings are grateful for their support.

The views expressed in this book are those of the author and should not be ascribed to any of the persons or organizations acknowledged above, or to the trustees, officers, or staff members of the Brookings Institution.

BRUCE K. MACLAURY
President

September 1994
Washington, D . C.

Contents

Preface to the Studies on Integrating National Economies

E CONOMIC interdependence among nations has increased sharply in the past half century. For example, while the value of total production of industrial countries increased at a rate of about 9 percent a year on average between 1964 and 1992, the value of the exports of those nations grew at an average rate of 12 percent, and lending and borrowing across national borders through banks surged upward even more rapidly at 23 percent a year. This international economic interdependence has contributed to significantly improved standards of living for most countries. Continuing international economic integration holds out the promise of further benefits. Yet the increasing sensitivity of national economies to events and policies originating abroad creates dilemmas and pitfalls if national policies and international cooperation are poorly managed.

The Brookings Project on Integrating National Economies, of which this study is a component, focuses on the interplay between two fundamental facts about the world at the end of the twentieth century. First, the world will continue for the foreseeable future to be organized politically into nation-states with sovereign governments. Second, increasing economic integration among nations will continue to erode differences among national economies and undermine the autonomy of national governments. The project explores the opportunities and tensions arising from these two facts.

Scholars from a variety of disciplines have produced twenty-one studies for the first phase of the project. Each study examines the heightened competition between national political sovereignty and increased cross-border economic integration. This preface identifies

xi

background themes and issues common to all the studies and provides a brief overview of the project as a whole.[1]

Increasing World Economic Integration

Two underlying sets of causes have led nations to become more closely intertwined. First, technological, social, and cultural changes have sharply reduced the effective economic distances among nations. Second, many of the government policies that traditionally inhibited cross-border transactions have been relaxed or even dismantled.

The same improvements in transportation and communications technology that make it much easier and cheaper for companies in New York to ship goods to California, for residents of Strasbourg to visit relatives in Marseilles, and for investors in Hokkaido to buy and sell shares on the Tokyo Stock Exchange facilitate trade, migration, and capital movements spanning nations and continents. The sharply reduced costs of moving goods, money, people, and information underlie the profound economic truth that technology has made the world markedly smaller.

New communications technology has been especially significant for financial activity. Computers, switching devices, and telecommunications satellites have slashed the cost of transmitting information internationally, of confirming transactions, and of paying for transactions. In the 1950s, for example, foreign exchange could be bought and sold only during conventional business hours in the initiating party's time zone. Such transactions can now be carried out instantaneously twenty-four hours a day. Large banks pass the management of their world-wide foreign-exchange positions around the globe from one branch to another, staying continuously ahead of the setting sun.

Such technological innovations have increased the knowledge of potentially profitable international exchanges and of economic opportunities abroad. Those developments, in turn, have changed consumers' and producers' tastes. Foreign goods, foreign vacations, foreign financial investments—virtually anything from other nations—have lost some of their exotic character.

1. A complete list of authors and study titles is included at the beginning of this volume, facing the title page.

Although technological change permits increased contact among nations, it would not have produced such dramatic effects if it had been countermanded by government policies. Governments have traditionally taxed goods moving in international trade, directly restricted imports and subsidized exports, and tried to limit international capital movements. Those policies erected "separation fences" at the borders of nations. From the perspective of private sector agents, separation fences imposed extra costs on cross-border transactions. They reduced trade and, in some cases, eliminated it. During the 1930s governments used such policies with particular zeal, a practice now believed to have deepened and lengthened the Great Depression.

After World War II, most national governments began—sometimes unilaterally, more often collaboratively—to lower their separation fences, to make them more permeable, or sometimes even to tear down parts of them. The multilateral negotiations under the auspices of the General Agreement on Trade and Tariffs (GATT)—for example, the Kennedy Round in the 1960s, the Tokyo Round in the 1970s, and most recently the protracted negotiations of the Uruguay Round, formally signed only in April 1994—stand out as the most prominent examples of fence lowering for trade in goods. Though contentious and marked by many compromises, the GATT negotiations are responsible for sharp reductions in at-the-border restrictions on trade in goods and services. After the mid-1980s a large number of developing countries moved unilaterally to reduce border barriers and to pursue outwardly oriented policies.

The lowering of fences for financial transactions began later and was less dramatic. Nonetheless, by the 1990s government restrictions on capital flows, especially among the industrial countries, were much less important and widespread than at the end of World War II and in the 1950s.

By shrinking the economic distances among nations, changes in technology would have progressively integrated the world economy even in the absence of reductions in governments' separation fences. Reductions in separation fences would have enhanced interdependence even without the technological innovations. Together, these two sets of evolutionary changes have reinforced each other and strikingly transformed the world economy.

Changes in the Government of Nations

Simultaneously with the transformation of the global economy, major changes have occurred in the world's political structure. First, the number of governmental decisionmaking units in the world has expanded markedly and political power has been diffused more broadly among them. Rising nationalism and, in some areas, heightened ethnic tensions have accompanied that increasing political pluralism.

The history of membership in international organizations documents the sharp growth in the number of independent states. For example, only 44 nations participated in the Bretton Woods conference of July 1944, which gave birth to the International Monetary Fund. But by the end of 1970, the IMF had 118 member nations. The number of members grew to 150 by the mid-1980s and to 178 by December 1993. Much of this growth reflects the collapse of colonial empires. Although many nations today are small and carry little individual weight in the global economy, their combined influence is considerable and their interests cannot be ignored as easily as they were in the past.

A second political trend, less visible but equally important, has been the gradual loss of the political and economic hegemony of the United States. Immediately after World War II, the United States by itself accounted for more than one-third of world production. By the early 1990s the U.S. share had fallen to about one-fifth. Concurrently, the political and economic influence of the European colonial powers continued to wane, and the economic significance of nations outside Europe and North America, such as Japan, Korea, Indonesia, China, Brazil, and Mexico, increased. A world in which economic power and influence are widely diffused has displaced a world in which one or a few nations effectively dominated international decisionmaking.

Turmoil and the prospect of fundamental change in the formerly centrally planned economies compose a third factor causing radical changes in world politics. During the era of central planning, governments in those nations tried to limit external influences on their economies. Now leaders in the formerly planned economies are trying to adopt reforms modeled on Western capitalist principles. To the extent that these efforts succeed, those nations will increase their economic involvement with the rest of the world. Political and economic alignments among the Western industrialized nations will be forced to adapt.

Governments and scholars have begun to assess these three trends, but their far-reaching ramifications will not be clear for decades.

Dilemmas for National Policies

Cross-border economic integration and national political sovereignty have increasingly come into conflict, leading to a growing mismatch between the economic and political structures of the world. The effective domains of economic markets have come to coincide less and less with national governmental jurisdictions.

When the separation fences at nations' borders were high, governments and citizens could sharply distinguish "international" from "domestic" policies. International policies dealt with at-the-border barriers, such as tariffs and quotas, or responded to events occurring abroad. In contrast, domestic policies were concerned with everything behind the nation's borders, such as competition and antitrust rules, corporate governance, product standards, worker safety, regulation and supervision of financial institutions, environmental protection, tax codes, and the government's budget. Domestic policies were regarded as matters about which nations were sovereign, to be determined by the preferences of the nation's citizens and its political institutions, without regard for effects on other nations.

As separation fences have been lowered and technological innovations have shrunk economic distances, a multitude of formerly neglected differences among nations' domestic policies have become exposed to international scrutiny. National governments and international negotiations must thus increasingly deal with "deeper"—behind-the-border—integration. For example, if country A permits companies to emit air and water pollutants whereas country B does not, companies that use pollution-generating methods of production will find it cheaper to produce in country A. Companies in country B that compete internationally with companies in country A are likely to complain that foreign competitors enjoy unfair advantages and to press for international pollution standards.

Deeper integration requires analysis of the economic and the political aspects of virtually all nonborder policies and practices. Such issues have already figured prominently in negotiations over the evolution of the European Community, over the Uruguay Round of GATT negotiations, over the North American Free Trade Agreement (NAFTA), and over the bilateral economic relationships between Japan and the United States. Future debates about behind-the-border policies will occur with increasing frequency and prove at least as complex and contentious as the past negotiations regarding at-the-border restrictions.

Tensions about deeper integration arise from three broad sources: cross-border spillovers, diminished national autonomy, and challenges to political sovereignty.

Cross-Border Spillovers

Some activities in one nation produce consequences that spill across borders and affect other nations. Illustrations of these spillovers abound. Given the impact of modern technology of banking and securities markets in creating interconnected networks, lax rules in one nation erode the ability of all other nations to enforce banking and securities rules and to deal with fraudulent transactions. Given the rapid diffusion of knowledge, science and technology policies in one nation generate knowledge that other nations can use without full payment. Labor market policies become matters of concern to other nations because workers migrate in search of work; policies in one nation can trigger migration that floods or starves labor markets elsewhere. When one nation dumps pollutants into the air or water that other nations breathe or drink, the matter goes beyond the unitary concern of the polluting nation and becomes a matter for international negotiation. Indeed, the hydrocarbons that are emitted into the atmosphere when individual nations burn coal for generating electricity contribute to global warming and are thereby a matter of concern for the entire world.

The tensions associated with cross-border spillovers can be especially vexing when national policies generate outcomes alleged to be competitively inequitable, as in the example in which country A permits companies to emit pollutants and country B does not. Or consider a situation in which country C requires commodities, whether produced at home or abroad, to meet certain design standards, justified for safety reasons. Foreign competitors may find it too expensive to meet these standards. In that event, the standards in C act very much like tariffs or quotas, effectively narrowing or even eliminating foreign competition for domestic producers. Citing examples of this sort, producers or governments in individual nations often complain that business is not conducted on a "level playing field." Typically, the complaining nation proposes that *other* nations adjust their policies to moderate or remove the competitive inequities.

Arguments for creating a level playing field are troublesome at best. International trade occurs precisely because of differences among nations—in resource endowments, labor skills, and consumer tastes. Nations specialize in producing goods and services in which they are relatively most efficient. In a fundamental sense, cross-border trade is valuable because the playing field is *not* level.

When David Ricardo first developed the theory of comparative advantage, he focused on differences among nations owing to climate or technology. But Ricardo could as easily have ascribed the productive differences to differing "social climates" as to physical or technological climates. Taking all "climatic" differences as given, the theory of comparative advantage argues that free trade among nations will maximize global welfare.

Taken to its logical extreme, the notion of leveling the playing field implies that nations should become homogeneous in all major respects. But that recommendation is unrealistic and even pernicious. Suppose country A decides that it is too poor to afford the costs of a clean environment, and will thus permit the production of goods that pollute local air and water supplies. Or suppose it concludes that it cannot afford stringent protections for worker safety. Country A will then argue that it is inappropriate for other nations to impute to country A the value they themselves place on a clean environment and safety standards (just as it would be inappropriate to impute the A valuations to the environment of other nations). The core of the idea of political sovereignty is to permit national residents to order their lives and property in accord with their own preferences.

Which perspective about differences among nations in behind-the-border policies is more compelling? Is country A merely exercising its national preferences and appropriately exploiting its comparative advantage in goods that are dirty or dangerous to produce? Or does a legitimate international problem exist that justifies pressure from other nations urging country A to accept changes in its policies (thus curbing its national sovereignty)? When national governments negotiate resolutions to such questions—trying to agree whether individual nations are legitimately exercising sovereign choices or, alternatively, engaging in behavior that is unfair or damaging to other nations—the dialogue is invariably contentious because the resolutions depend on the typically complex circumstances of the international spillovers and on the relative weights accorded to the interests of particular individuals and particular nations.

Diminished National Autonomy

As cross-border economic integration increases, governments experience greater difficulties in trying to control events within their borders. Those difficulties, summarized by the term *diminished autonomy*, are the second set of reasons why tensions arise from the competition between political sovereignty and economic integration.

For example, nations adjust monetary and fiscal policies to influence domestic inflation and employment. In setting these policies, smaller countries have always been somewhat constrained by foreign economic events and policies. Today, however, all nations are constrained, often severely. More than in the past, therefore, nations may be better able to achieve their economic goals if they work together collaboratively in adjusting their macroeconomic policies.

Diminished autonomy and cross-border spillovers can sometimes be allowed to persist without explicit international cooperation to deal with them. States in the United States adopt their own tax systems and set policies for assistance to poor single people without any formal cooperation or limitation. Market pressures operate to force a degree of de facto cooperation. If one state taxes corporations too heavily, it knows business will move elsewhere. (Those familiar with older debates about "fiscal federalism" within the United States and other nations will recognize the similarity between those issues and the emerging international debates about deeper integration of national economies.) Analogously, differences among nations in regulations, standards, policies, institutions, and even social and cultural preferences create economic incentives for a kind of arbitrage that erodes or eliminates the differences. Such pressures involve not only the conventional arbitrage that exploits price differentials (buying at one point in geographic space or time and selling at another) but also shifts in the location of production facilities and in the residence of factors of production.

In many other cases, however, cross-border spillovers, arbitrage pressures, and diminished effectiveness of national policies can produce unwanted consequences. In cases involving what economists call externalities (external economies and diseconomies), national governments may need to cooperate to promote mutual interests. For example, population growth, continued urbanization, and the more intensive exploitation of natural resources generate external diseconomies not only within but across national boundaries. External economies generated when benefits spill across national jurisdictions probably also increase in importance (for instance, the gains from basic research and from control of communicable diseases).

None of these situations is new, but technological change and the reduction of tariffs and quotas heighten their importance. When one nation produces goods (such as scientific research) or "bads" (such as pollution) that significantly affect other nations, individual governments acting sequentially and noncooperatively cannot deal effectively with the resulting issues. In the absence of explicit cooperation and political leadership, too few collective goods and too many collective bads will be supplied.

Challenges to Political Sovereignty

The pressures from cross-border economic integration sometimes even lead individuals or governments to challenge the core assumptions of national political sovereignty. Such challenges are a third source of tensions about deeper integration.

The existing world system of nation-states assumes that a nation's residents are free to follow their own values and to select their own political arrangements without interference from others. Similarly, property rights are allocated by nation. (The so-called global commons, such as outer space and the deep seabed, are the sole exceptions.) A nation is assumed to have the sovereign right to exploit its property in accordance with its own preferences and policies. Political sovereignty is thus analogous to the concept of consumer sovereignty (the presumption that the individual consumer best knows his or her own interests and should exercise them freely).

In times of war, some nations have had sovereignty wrested from them by force. In earlier eras, a handful of individuals or groups have questioned the premises of political sovereignty. With the profound increases in economic integration in recent decades, however, a larger number of individuals and groups—and occasionally even their national governments—have identified circumstances in which, it is claimed, some universal or international set of values should take precedence over the preferences or policies of particular nations.

Some groups seize on human-rights issues, for example, or what they deem to be egregiously inappropriate political arrangements in other nations. An especially prominent case occurred when citizens in many nations labeled the former apartheid policies of South Africa an affront to universal values and emphasized that the South African government was not legitimately representing the interests of a majority of South Africa's residents. Such views caused many national governments to apply economic sanctions against South Africa. Examples of value conflicts are not restricted to human rights, however. Groups focusing on environmental issues characterize tropical rain forests as the lungs of the world and the genetic repository for numerous species of plants and animals that are the heritage of all mankind. Such views lead Europeans, North Americans, or Japanese to challenge the timber-cutting policies of Brazilians and Indonesians. A recent controversy over tuna fishing with long drift nets that kill porpoises is yet another example. Environmentalists in the United States whose sensibilities were offended by the drowning of porpoises required U.S. boats at some additional expense to amend their fishing practices. The U.S. fishermen, complaining about imported tuna caught with less regard for porpoises, persuaded the U.S. government to ban such tuna imports (both direct imports from the countries in which the tuna is caught and indirect imports shipped via third countries). Mexico and Venezuela were the main countries affected by this ban; a GATT dispute panel sided with Mexico against the United States in the controversy, which further upset the U.S. environmental community.

A common feature of all such examples is the existence, real or alleged, of "psychological externalities" or "political failures." Those holding such views reject untrammeled political sovereignty for nation-states in deference to universal or non-national values. They wish to constrain the exercise of individual nations' sovereignties through international negotiations or, if necessary, by even stronger intervention.

The Management of International Convergence

In areas in which arbitrage pressures and cross-border spillovers are weak and psychological or political externalities are largely absent, national governments may encounter few problems with deeper integration. Diversity across nations may persist quite easily. But at the other extreme, arbitrage and spillovers in some areas may be so strong that they threaten to erode national diversity completely. Or psychological and political sensitivities may be asserted too powerfully to be ignored. Governments will then be confronted with serious tensions, and national policies and behaviors may eventually converge to common, worldwide patterns (for example, subject to internationally agreed norms or minimum standards). Eventual convergence across nations, if it occurs, could happen in a harmful way (national policies and practices being driven to a least common denominator with externalities ignored, in effect a "race to the bottom") or it could occur with mutually beneficial results ("survival of the fittest and the best").

Each study in this series addresses basic questions about the management of international convergence: if, when, and how national governments should intervene to try to influence the consequences of arbitrage pressures, cross-border spillovers, diminished autonomy, and the assertion of psychological or political externalities. A wide variety of responses is conceivable. We identify six, which should be regarded not as distinct categories but as ranges along a continuum.

National autonomy defines a situation at one end of the continuum in which national governments make decentralized decisions with little or no consultation and no explicit cooperation. This response represents political sovereignty at its strongest, undiluted by any international management of convergence.

Mutual recognition, like national autonomy, presumes decentralized decisions by national governments and relies on market competition to guide the process of international convergence. Mutual recognition, however, entails exchanges of information and consultations among governments to constrain the formation of national regulations and policies. As understood in discussions of economic integration within the European Community, moreover, mutual recognition entails an explicit acceptance by each member nation of the regulations, standards, and certification procedures of other members. For example, mutual recognition allows wine or liquor produced in any European Union country to be sold in all twelve member countries even if production standards in member countries differ. Doctors licensed in France are permitted to practice in Germany, and vice versa, even if licensing procedures in the two countries differ.

Governments may agree on rules that restrict their freedom to set policy or that promote gradual convergence in the structure of policy. As international consultations and monitoring of compliance with such rules become more important, this situation can be described as *monitored decentralization*. The Group of Seven finance ministers meetings, supplemented by the IMF's surveillance over exchange rate and macroeconomic policies, illustrate this approach to management.

Coordination goes further than mutual recognition and monitored decentralization in acknowledging convergence pressures. It is also more ambitious in promoting intergovernmental cooperation to deal with them. Coordination involves jointly designed mutual adjustments of national policies. In clear-cut cases of coordination, bargaining occurs and governments agree to behave differently from the ways they would have behaved without the agreement. Examples include the World Health Organization's procedures for controlling communicable diseases and the 1987 Montreal Protocol (to a 1985 framework convention) for the protection of stratospheric ozone by reducing emissions of chlorofluorocarbons.

Explicit harmonization, which requires still higher levels of intergovernmental cooperation, may require agreement on regional standards or world standards. Explicit harmonization typically entails still greater departures from decentralization in decisionmaking and still further strengthening of international institutions. The 1988 agreement among major central banks to set minimum standards for the required capital positions of commercial banks (reached through the Committee on Banking Regulations and Supervisory Practices at the Bank for International Settlements) is an example of partially harmonized regulations.

At the opposite end of the spectrum from national autonomy lies *federalist mutual governance*, which implies continuous bargaining and joint, centralized decisionmaking. To make federalist mutual governance work would require greatly strengthened supranational institutions. This end of the management spectrum, now relevant only as an analytical benchmark, is a possible outcome that can be imagined for the middle or late decades of the twenty-first century, possibly even sooner for regional groupings like the European Union.

Overview of the Brookings Project

Despite their growing importance, the issues of deeper economic integration and its competition with national political sovereignty were largely neglected in the 1980s. In 1992 the Brookings Institution initiated its project on Integrating National Economies to direct attention to these important questions.

In studying this topic, Brookings sought and received the co-operation of some of the world's leading economists, political scientists, foreign-policy specialists, and government officials, representing all regions of the world. Although some functional areas require a special focus on European, Japanese, and North American perspectives, at all junctures the goal was to include, in addition, the perspectives of developing nations and the formerly centrally planned economies.

The first phase of the project commissioned the twenty-one scholarly studies listed at the beginning of the book. One or two lead discussants, typically residents of parts of the world other than the area where the author resides, were asked to comment on each study.

Authors enjoyed substantial freedom to design their individual studies, taking due account of the overall themes and goals of the project. The guidelines for the studies requested that at least some of the analysis be carried out with a non-normative perspective. In effect, authors were asked to develop a "baseline" of what might happen in the absence of changed policies or further international cooperation. For their normative analyses, authors were asked to start with an agnostic posture that did not prejudge the net benefits or costs resulting from integration. The project organizers themselves had no presumption about whether national diversity is better or worse than international convergence or about what the individual studies should conclude regarding the desirability of increased integration. On the contrary, each author was asked to address the trade-offs in his or her issue area between diversity and convergence and to locate the area, currently and prospectively, on the spectrum of international management possibilities running between national autonomy through mutual recognition to coordination and explicit harmonization.

HENRY J. AARON   SUSAN M. COLLINS
RALPH C. BRYANT   ROBERT Z. LAWRENCE

Chapter 1

Economic Reform without Political Reform

C HINA'S transformation from a virtually closed economy to a major trading nation is a success story that has attracted wide attention. Since introducing its policies to open the economy in 1979, the People's Republic of China (PRC) has increased its exports at an average annual rate of 16.1 percent, and the country is now the tenth largest exporter in the world. Imports also have grown, at more than 15 percent a year. Annual growth rates for China's total trade were more than three times the world rates between 1978 and 1990.[1] In 1993, according to Chinese sources, China's foreign trade constituted 38 percent of its gross domestic product, an exceptionally high trade ratio for a country with such a large domestic market.[2] This flow of trade represents a huge expansion from the previous trickle of 10 percent in 1978. A major spur to this growth in trade has been the change in policy to welcome foreign investment to China. In 1978 China had no foreign direct investment; by 1993 China had attracted almost $60 billion of foreign in-

---

1. Lardy (1994, pp. 30–37); (1992b, p. 11).
2. "Wu Yi Questioned on 'Foreign Trade Law,'" Xinhua News Agency, May 13, 1994, in Foreign Broadcast Information Service, *Daily Report: China*, May 16, 1994, p. 27. (Hereafter FBIS, *China*.) This figure should be treated skeptically because China's gross domestic product is widely believed to be underestimated, and trade volume is overestimated by including at full value the exports produced from imported inputs. For a good discussion of the difficulty of estimating trade ratios in China, see Lardy (1994).

1

vestment in over 70,000 enterprises.[3] According to a World Bank economist, by 1993 China was receiving more foreign direct investment and new commercial bank credits than any other developing country.[4] (See the Appendix for additional data.)

China's effort to promote foreign trade and investment has been an integral part of its overall reform strategy since 1979. Foreign trade and investment have undoubtedly improved the country's economic performance during this period of reform. Joint ventures with foreign companies accounted for more than 27.5 percent of the country's exports in 1993, and during the first four months of 1994 the ratio rose to 36.9 percent.[5] Competition with joint ventures and foreign firms has induced Chinese firms to improve their efficiency and modernize their production technologies. Access to foreign managerial know-how and technology has made such modernization possible. The availability of imported consumer goods, albeit limited, has improved work incentives and moderated inflationary pressures by absorbing surplus currency.[6]

The policies to open the economy also have built political momentum behind the domestic reform drive. New opportunities and incentives for officials and managers to do business with foreigners have diluted their dependence on government planning and reoriented their preferences toward the market. By becoming a joint venture, an enterprise could escape the government plan

3. Lardy (1994, p. 63, table 3.7), value actually invested as of September 1993. The year 1993 saw a foreign investment boom in China. At the end of 1992 the accumulated figure was $34.16 billion. Wu Yi, *Guoji Shangbao*, April 15, 1993, p. 1, in FBIS, *China*, May 18, 1993, p. 37.) World Bank (1994, p. xvi) gives the figure of $58.1 billion (contracted value) of foreign investment in more than 90,000 projects.

4. The information is drawn from a quotation by Michael Bruno, former chief economist of the World Bank, in a press conference as reported in "World Bank Reports on Foreign Investment in China," Xinhua News Agency, December 15, 1993, in FBIS, *China*, December 16, 1993, p. 4. According to the source, total foreign resources flows to China during 1993 were projected to reach $27 billion ($15 billion in direct foreign investment, $5 billion in portfolio investment, $3.5 billion from other private sources, $2.5 billion in official loans and grants, and $1 billion from commercial banks).

5. "Excessively Rapid Growth by Foreign-Funded Enterprises Will Adversely Affect Foreign Exchange Market," *Ming Pao* (Hong Kong), March 4, 1994, p. A12, in FBIS, *China*, March 24, 1994, p. 52; "Customs Reports Exports Growing Faster than Imports," Xinhua News Agency, May 16, 1994, in FBIS, *China*, May 18, 1994, p. 56.

6. Liu Dizhong, "Imports of Consumer Goods Increased to Soak Up Excess Money," *China Daily*, April 25, 1985, p. 1, in Joint Publications Research Service, *China Economic Affairs*, 85-049, May 29, 1985, pp. 95–96.

and make much more money producing for the market. Thousands of joint ventures have swelled the ranks of private and collectively owned businesses pressing for market freedoms. As this nonstate sector grew—it now produces approximately 50 percent of total industrial output—it reduced the stultifying dominance of the state-owned economy. The foreign firms and governments doing business in China became an influential voice in the reform coalition. During periods of economic overheating, when a conservative domestic backlash threatened to recentralize control, foreign investors showed displeasure by keeping their money in their pockets and investigating alternative sites in Southeast Asia and Mexico. Feeling the pressure, Beijing soon returned to the path of reform. China's labor-intensive light industries and the coastal provinces where such industries are concentrated, previously neglected by communist economic policies, grew in influence as the source of most of the country's export earnings and put their weight behind the reform drive.

Even now, however, although its volume of foreign trade and investment has increased dramatically, China's economy is only shallowly integrated into the world economy, according to the "relaxation of at-the-border restrictions" definition of shallow integration proposed by the editors of the series on integrating national economies, of which this book is a part.[7] As of 1994 China's domestic market remains protected, only some enterprises are allowed to trade directly with foreigners, exports are subsidized, and the currency is not yet convertible. State control over trading activities, although no longer total as it was under central planning, continues to be extensive, and decisions about who gets to share the benefits of foreign trade and investment are selective and highly politicized. As Deputy U.S. Trade Representative Charlene Barshefsky described it, "China's import regime still remains the creature of central planners and state bureaucrats."[8] Analysts of the country depict its trading system as retaining some characteristics of the planned economy, such as foreign trade monopo-

7. See the preface to this volume.
8. Carol Goldstein, "Join the Club," *Far Eastern Economic Review*, March 17, 1994, p. 43.

lies, import licenses and control, and high customs tariffs, and point out that this kind of administrative control of foreign trade is a major source of corruption.[9] The issues currently facing China in its international economic relations are those that would perpetuate shallow integration, namely, reforming the foreign exchange regime and lowering import barriers.

China has not yet confronted the challenge of deep integration, defined by the series editors in the preface as nonborder policies once deemed purely domestic matters, such as competition and antitrust policies, technology policies, product standards, worker safety standards, environmental standards, corporate governance rules, regulation and supervision of financial institutions, tax policies, and monetary and budgetary policies. Only one issue of deep integration, intellectual property rights, has been addressed in legislation by China in response to U.S. pressure. International demands on China regarding deep integration issues like labor and environmental standards are on the horizon, however. The prison labor issue has already entered into U.S.-China trade relations; and because of the scale, severity, and global effects of its industrial pollution, China is becoming a prime target for the world's environmentalists.

This book tells the story of how China ended its long-held policies of economic isolationism and rejoined the world economy in the decade and a half between 1979 and 1994. What is most remarkable about China's takeoff as a world trading power is that it was achieved without any major alteration in the country's communist political system. China achieved economic reform without political reform. The very same Communist Party and government institutions that for thirty years walled off China from the world economy opened the door. How was such a turnaround possible? Why could it occur in China but not in the Soviet Union?

This analysis looks for answers in politics instead of economics. Economists often view China's post-1979 open policy as its leaders' rational response to the inefficiencies of the previous autarkic

---

9. "Report on Interview with Hu Angang and Kang Xiaoguang," *Ming Pao* (Hong Kong), February 4, 1994, p. A10, in FBIS, *China,* February 15, FBIS, 1994, p. 16.

command economy.[10] Economists' interpretations of the reforms, however, do not provide an adequate explanation of the specific form and content of reform policies or the different outcomes in China and the Soviet Union, which have a political rather than economic basis.

The success of China's opening presents an anomaly that contradicts common understandings about how political institutions perpetuate economic policies. In all countries, political institutions are designed to tilt policy choice in a certain direction. Institutions raise the odds that certain policies will be adopted by giving the groups who benefit from these policies disproportionate influence in the policymaking process. Once entrenched in institutions, groups with vested interests in existing policies use their political authority to resist policy change. Communist institutions were established in China during the 1950s to emulate the rapid industrialization policies of the Soviet Union by creating a closed centrally planned economy, protecting heavy industries from international competition, and redistributing resources from coastal regions toward more backward inland ones. Under these institutional arrangements, central Communist Party and government officials, economic planners, heavy industries and the ministries that represent them, and inland provinces came to have substantial political clout and an obvious stake in perpetuating a closed command economy.

Therefore the puzzle is why China's leaders promoted economic reform, how they were able to win support for reform policies among Communist Party and government officials, and why they adopted particular reform policies such as special economic zones, foreign trade contracting, and dual-track currency exchange. The premise is that one should study policymaking in communist countries much as one would in democracies: by focusing on the competition among politicians who operate in an institutionalized political setting. Scholars of policymaking in democracies analyze the way electoral, legislative, and executive powers and procedures

10. Perkins (1991, p. 269).

create political incentives for politicians and set the rules for collective choice. Different institutional arrangements generate distinctive political incentives and choice rules and produce predictable policy outcomes.

Scholars of communist systems usually ignore the institutional framework of policymaking. They assume that institutional rules and lines of authority are irrelevant and that all decisions are made by a few top leaders. In fact, policymaking in China is a pluralistic process involving hundreds of officials; and although the informal power of a few top leaders like Deng Xiaoping still influences policy choices, the formal and tacit rules of Chinese politics also shape these choices. The authority to choose top Communist Party leaders, granted by the party constitution to the Central Committee, and the party's legal authority to appoint government officials set the context in which Chinese officials compete for career advancement and make policies. Because communist regimes like China lack an open sphere of political competition (elections), competition for leadership posts occurs within the bureaucracy and is intertwined with policymaking in a distinctive pattern T. H. Rigby has called "crypto-politics."[11] In the absence of fixed terms of office, competition for leadership is constant, with the struggle for power intensifying when the incumbent top leader is elderly or obviously weak, as has been the case during the entire post-1979 era of economic reform in China.

My story offers an answer to the question of why China, unlike the Soviet Union, was able to accomplish economic reform without political reform, namely, that China's version of communism was less well institutionalized and more decentralized than the USSR's. The fact that China's system was more primitive, that is, less institutionalized and less centralized, proved to be an advantage in setting its economy on a new course. My analysis of the political logic of Chinese institutions also illuminates the distinctive features of China's path of reform—gradualism, administrative decentralization, and particularistic contracting—and explains why this path will not automatically lead to an open domestic market, a convertible currency, or deep integration with the world

11. Rigby (1964).

economy. The logic of domestic politics in China that made possible partial opening and shallow integration will not automatically push the door open further, much less produce harmonization with international standards for intellectual property, labor, and the environment. International pressure and changed group preferences within China, however, are combining to move China toward greater openness and deeper international integration.

In the 1960s and 1970s the so-called Chinese model of self-reliant, egalitarian, rural-based economic modernization was widely touted. Now that even the Chinese themselves acknowledge the failure of their previous development strategy, China offers a new and very different model to the world, a model of economic marketization and internationalization under authoritarian rule. People in countries like the Democratic People's Republic of Korea, Vietnam, and Cuba, as well as other non-communist state-dominated economies that admire China's success, may find my analysis helpful for understanding the political practicability of the new Chinese model.

Chapter 2

The Pre-reform System: The Closed Command Economy

WHEN the Communist Party came to power in China, it copied its development strategy and its economic and political institutions from the Soviet Union, the only other large communist country available as a model. Once the development strategy of rapid capital-intensive industrialization centered on steel and machinery was chosen, an import-substitution trade regime naturally followed.[1] To achieve the goal of a self-reliant industrial economy, domestic industry was protected from foreign competition by direct controls on imports and investment and administrative allocation of foreign exchange combined with an overvalued currency. These policies, enforced by central planners and a central foreign trade monopoly, built an airtight wall between the domestic economy and the world economy. Only the central foreign trade ministry and its twelve trade corporations were permitted to engage in trading activities; everyone else was isolated from foreign business.

The foreign trade plan was treated as an addendum to the domestic plan, which was calculated by balancing material inputs and outputs. Practically the only imports allowed were capital goods to accelerate China's rapid industrialization or to satisfy demand that could not be met domestically because of the shortages congenital to the centrally planned economy. Imports consisted mainly of industrial equipment, most notably 166 industrial plants imported from the Soviet Union during the First Five-Year

---

1. Perkins (1968, p. 187); Lardy (1992b, p. 5).

8

Plan (1953–58) and a smaller number of synthetic fiber and chemical fertilizer plants imported from Japan and the West during the 1960s and 1970s.[2] During the early 1960s, food imports mitigated the famine created by the Great Leap Forward, and imports of chemical fertilizer promoted agricultural recovery .

Exports were viewed as a way to finance imports. Because domestic prices were set by the state and bore no relation to world prices or to real scarcities, foreign trade officials had no way to determine the most efficient mix of exports and simply exported the goods that exceeded planned domestic demand, mainly agricultural and primary goods.[3]

Many of the features of the Soviet-style command economy adopted by China were designed to concentrate resources for rapid growth of heavy industry. Centralized planning and allocation of industrial labor, material inputs, finance, output, and distribution guaranteed that heavy industry had the first claim on resources. Administratively set prices—low for agricultural products and high for industrial ones—extracted resources from the rural areas to invest in urban industry and kept urban food prices low. The agricultural commune system helped suppress rural consumption levels in order to squeeze savings, sometimes as high as 30 percent of GNP, to invest in industry. A public finance system based on revenues from the profits of state factories tied the interests of the central state to the system of rich industry and poor agriculture. Controls on internal migration kept hordes of disadvantaged peasants from flooding the cities. The closed command economy protected the holders of scarce capital, particularly the central state and its heavy industrial ministries. Other beneficiaries were the inland provinces, more backward and inward-looking than the coast, which were favored in Beijing's investment policies;[4] the military, which produced a large share of heavy

2. Lardy (1992b, p. 30). Cumings (1979) argues that China's import-substitution trade policy stopped with the Sino-Soviet split in 1960, but Lardy (1992b, p. 31) sees more continuity right up to 1979.

3. The share of primary products in China's exports fell from almost 80 percent in 1953 to 64 percent in 1957 and then 56 percent in 1965–66 and remained roughly constant at that level for the rest of the 1960s and 1970s. Lardy (1992b, p. 32).

4. Lardy (1978); Naughton (1988).

equipment like ships, trucks, and airplanes;[5] and the Communist Party agencies, whose raison d'être was social and economic control.[6]

The losers were the agricultural and light industrial sectors, which were blocked from exploiting the international comparative advantage offered by China's abundant, well-educated labor in world markets. Consumers, both urban and rural, were harmed by the administrative suppression of consumption levels and the denial of access to foreign consumer goods. It can be argued that the opportunity costs of the closed economy increased to these groups after the early 1970s, when the expansion of international markets raised the demand for China's labor-intensive goods.[7] The groups disadvantaged by autarky constituted an overwhelming majority of China's population (agricultural employment alone constituted 80 percent). Yet the authoritarian institutions that isolated China from the world prevented these groups from realizing what they could have gained from opening up. Even if they had been aware of the potential gains, without elections they had no mechanism for influencing national policies.

The Soviet-style command of resources enabled China to achieve high rates of industrial growth, estimated at approximately 10 percent annually from 1949 to 1980. Between the two peak years of 1953 and 1978, there was 6 percent average annual growth of the net material product.[8] The inefficiency of the economic system, however, meant that more and more capital and labor had to be pumped into industry to sustain high growth. One estimate is that total factor productivity declined between the early 1950s and 1979 at an average annual rate of 2.75 percent.[9] Nevertheless, there was nothing inevitable about the Chinese leaders' move to launch an economic reform drive in late 1978. China was not experiencing an economic crisis, and indeed the economy was operating more efficiently than the Soviet economy. Mao's chosen successor, Hua Guofeng, had already decided to take advantage of

5. Lardy (1992b, p. 23) notes that the military received preferential treatment in all of its trading activities.

6. See Shirk (1984) on the "communist coalition" of groups favored by the closed command economy.

7. See Frieden and Rogowski (forthcoming).

8. Naughton (1989, pp. 228).

9. Dernberger (1981).

the rise in world oil prices by promoting petroleum exports and importing more high-tech turnkey plants. Chinese economic performance and living standards could have been substantially improved by minor adjustments in the economic system, such as modernizing planning methods, shifting factory decisionmaking from party secretaries to managers, evaluating managers on the basis of long-term performance including profits, introducing a labor market and piecework bonuses, or increasing agricultural investment. All of these had already been tried in the Soviet Union to good effect. China, unlike the Soviet Union, had not reached the limits of the extensive growth development strategy before reforms. It was still a predominantly agricultural country with massive reserves of labor. Increased exports, although desirable, were not essential because of the large scale of the domestic market. With a more technically sound system of planning and work incentives, the Chinese economy could have continued to grow. Deng Xiaoping's decision to introduce reforms in late 1978 was dictated not by economic necessity, but by Deng's political interest in discrediting Hua Guofeng and seizing the reins of power from him.[10] Competition for party leadership provided the opening for policy innovation.

10. For an argument about why Deng's 1978 reform initiative was driven by the logic of leadership succession competition, see Shirk (forthcoming).

Chapter 3

China's Political Institutions

*T*HE decision to open China to the world and launch market reforms was primarily Deng Xiaoping's. Despite China's decentralized economic administration and the reciprocal relationship between leaders and the bureaucratic elite (see below), the top leader in the Chinese Communist Party holds immense authority. Deng Xiaoping's personal commitment to economic opening and marketization and his artful political leadership have had much to do not just with launching the reform drive, but also with sustaining it in the face of continued attacks from threatened bureaucratic interests.

The genius of Deng Xiaoping, however, cannot explain the success of Chinese reforms or their distinctive pattern. Deng Xiaoping pushed the economy in the general direction of greater openness and more unit autonomy, competition, and material incentives, but specific policies had to be hammered out by groups of officials in party and government arenas. Other scholars have previously noted that Chinese policymaking is a pluralistic process with power fragmented among various bureaucratic levels and departments.[1] My objective is to take the analysis of policymaking beyond the insight of "fragmented authoritarianism" by specifying the institutional structure that shapes this pluralistic policy process.

---

1. Lieberthal and Oksenberg (1988); Lampton (1987b).

Who's in Charge? The Communist Party and the Government

The authority relationship between the Chinese Communist Party (CCP) and the government is at the core of all communist political systems.[2] The party has ultimate authority. Party officials do not have to stand for election, and the party is not formally accountable to citizens. Influence over the policy process is closed to citizens and limited to officials; as a result the benefits of policy are also concentrated on officials. Although legislatures exist at every level, they have no actual authority. In the absence of elected legislatures that represent regional interests, China's economically dynamic and populous coastal provinces are deprived of a political voice that matches their economic and demographic strength. Without elections, China's rural majority is disenfranchised and politically powerless.[3] The rural population is also underrepresented within the party membership and its leading organs, and the government agencies that represent the interests of rural agriculture are weak (see below).

Like any principal in a large organization, the Communist Party has limited information and therefore delegates much policymaking and all administration to the government bureaucracy, which has more expert and specialized information. In the language of institutional economics, the party is the principal and the government the agent. The party's authority over the government is based primarily on its *nomenklatura* power, the power to appoint and promote government officials. The party also sets the general policy line and approves the government budget and plan. The relationship between party committees and government departments is one of direct subordination, even when they are at the same administrative level.

The Communist Party's political dominance over the government made economic reforms possible. Party leaders had the power to prod the bureaucracy to action. With their vested interests in the command economy, central government planners and

2. This section summarizes information from chapters 3–7 of Shirk (1993).

3. For a persuasive argument on the urban bias of nonelectoral systems, see Bates (1981).

14   China's Political Institutions

ministry bureaucrats were unlikely to take bold initiatives on their own. Once party leaders made reform the official line, it was impossible for anyone inside or outside the government to oppose reform openly. And by replacing thousands of poorly educated or conservative government officials at all levels, the party eliminated roadblocks to reform.

Communist Party leaders oversee the work of government officials by the intensive method of "parallel rule":[4] the party selects all government officials; virtually all government officials are party members; and in each government department, party members report to a party committee that is subordinate to higher-level party committees. Through a hierarchy of party committees parallel to the hierarchy of government departments, party cadres oversee government operations from within the government, not from outside. This system of constant, tight monitoring was designed by the Soviets and adopted by the Chinese and other communist systems as a solution to the problem of supervising officials from the regime they have overthrown. It reflects mistrust of administrative discretion.

China took the method of parallel rule further than the Soviets did.[5] Within industrial enterprises, the CCP also exercised more intensive control than the Soviets ever had. Chinese party secretaries told managers what to do; Soviet party secretaries gave managers full managerial responsibility under the slogan "one-man management."

In the Chinese version of parallel rule, the organizational lines between party and government blurred, and the informational

4. McCubbins and Schwartz (1984) call this kind of constant monitoring of administrative action "police patrol oversight" and contrast it with "fire-alarm oversight," by which politicians establish a system of rules, procedures, and informal practices that enable citizen interest groups to check up on administrative actions. Because the political demobilization of the population is a fundamental requirement of communist systems, fire-alarm oversight is not an option.

5. Party groups (*dang zu*) (sometimes called party fractions or party core groups) were established in government agencies and took over decisionmaking within the agency. Party groups originated in the Soviet Union but came to play a more important role in China. Party groups in central government ministries are more powerful than the party committees; they are appointed by the party Organization Department, while the committees are theoretically elected; party committees have jurisdiction only over the party members in the ministry, while party groups have jurisdiction over even nonparty personnel and the entire vertical bureaucracy below the ministry.

advantages of delegation were lost. Poorly educated veteran party officials made policy decisions on the basis of political instincts rather than technical knowledge. Party members serving in government agencies were promoted more for political loyalty than for professional accomplishment.[6] Frequent party-led ideological campaigns against government officials whose behavior was defined as deviant made bureaucrats afraid of taking action.

During the decade of economic reform in China, party leaders delegated more discretion to the government in economic policymaking. Putting the government on a longer leash but keeping the leash in the party's grip was a way to raise the quality of decisions and the performance of the economy. It also was a way to make an end run around some conservative party leaders and tilt policymaking in the direction of reform. Government ministries and provinces were allowed to deliberate on policies, so those that were adopted were acceptable to key sectors and regions.

Within the Chinese government, institutions are structured to encourage advocacy of departmental interests and perspectives. Ministry and province officials, as appointees of the CCP, know that they cannot deviate too far from the preferences of CCP leaders, yet they are expected to articulate the interests of their particular sector or region in policy deliberations. The structure of the government bureaucracy affords virtual, that is, nonelectoral, representation to economic groups. Economic sectors do not have to lobby from outside the government because their interests are reflected in the positions taken by officials in their affiliated ministries. The economic reforms that allowed ministries and provincial departments to claim several percentage points of enterprise profits or foreign exchange earnings intensified the motivation of officials to press for policies favorable to their industry or region. As a result, reform policymaking was characterized by fierce intrabureaucratic contention.

When they established their government in the 1950s, Communist Party leaders created a structure that enhanced the clout of industrial producers. The State Council had approximately fifteen ministries for heavy industry (one-third of them managed by the

6. Harding (1981).

People's Liberation Army), but only a few devoted to agriculture or light industry. According to interviews, the most capable and respected officials were assigned to the heavy industrial ministries. Ownership and public finance arrangements also privileged heavy industry. Heavy industries "owned" most of their factories and ran them directly from Beijing, while light industrial and textile factories were placed under local governments, and farms were collectively owned and managed. The public finance system based on enterprise profits reinforced a policy bias of rich industry and poor agriculture. Whenever a proposal threatened to diminish industrial profits, the ministries had the influential Ministry of Finance on their side in blocking it.

Chinese communist institutions, modeled largely on those in the Soviet Union, privileged the interests of the central state over regional interests, even though the Chinese delegated a substantial degree of de facto autonomy to provincial and municipal governments (see below). Provincial governments had no institutional voice in Beijing, and unlike industrial interests, had to lobby from outside the State Council bureaucracy. To remedy this imbalance favoring central ministries over local governments, the reformist party leadership later expanded the arena for economic policymaking. Most reform policies were deliberated in large work conferences that included provincial representatives as well as ministry ones.

The CCP's pervasive control over the government means that delegation of economic decisionmaking is risk free for the party. The party's power over bureaucratic careers guarantees that officials will not "cross the shadowy line between advocacy and pressure."[7] Parallel rule enables party authorities to participate from within government agencies in setting agency positions. The party, by establishing a particular set of government agencies and calling work conferences, has determined who gets to sit around the bargaining table. And the Politburo can always veto government policies. Such vetoes are extremely rare, however, because career-minded government officials anticipate the reactions of party leaders to their actions.

---

7. Brzezinski and Huntington (1964, p. 196).

Reciprocal Accountability and Leadership Competition

In democratic systems the political incentives of politicians are shaped by the electoral connection: politicians take policy positions that will win them votes from their constituents. Although communist leaders are not popularly elected, neither are they absolute dictators, exempt from all accountability toward others. The lines of accountability, however, are more elusive in authoritarian regimes than in democracies; leadership selection processes are opaque and the formal rules for selection are not always followed.

Communist Party leaders (the General Secretary, Politburo, and Standing Committee of the Politburo) are chosen by what might be called a "selectorate," a term adopted from British parliamentary politics to define the group within a political party that has effective power to choose leaders. The Chinese selectorate, as prescribed by the party constitution, is the Central Committee, a body of approximately 200 that is chosen by the party Congress (a body of approximately 2,000 that meets every five years) and consists of party and government officials from the center, localities, and the military. In the Soviet Union, the authority of the Communist Party Central Committee to select leaders was firmly established in 1957, when Nikita Khrushchev defeated an attempt by the Standing Committee of the Politburo to depose him by winning the support of a Central Committee meeting, and in 1964, when the Central Committee did oust Khrushchev.[8]

In China, however, informal power continues to play a more influential role in leadership selection than it did in the Soviet Union. Senior party figures who are not members of the Central

8. "Any serious student of the structure of power in the Soviet Union before the summer of 1990 would have focused on the role of the Central Committee—the plenum of the Central Committee, as Soviets would express it. Although Westerners often said incorrectly that the Politburo was the focus of power in the old system, the only institution that could elect or replace a General Secretary—or any Politburo member—was the Central Committee. Whoever controlled a majority of the voting members of the Central Committee controlled the Politburo and the rest of the political system. Normally the loyalty of the Central Committee to the General Secretary was taken for granted by any potential challenger and, therefore, not tested, but a General Secretary who did not continually worry about that loyalty courted the fate that befell Nikita Khrushchev in October 1964." Hough (1991, p. 95).

Committee or Politburo continue to participate in selection decisions behind the scenes and sometimes attend enlarged meetings of the Politburo and Central Committee. The weakly institutionalized process of leadership selection within the CCP is illustrated in the three rounds of competition since Mao Zedong's death in 1976. In two instances, the firing of party general secretaries Hua Guofeng in 1980 and Zhao Ziyang in 1989, the Central Committee met and approved the Politburo's recommendation, but general secretary Hu Yaobang was fired in 1987 by an enlarged meeting of the Politburo, a decision not ratified by a Central Committee meeting.[9] Despite the continuing influence of the party elders, the younger generation of Chinese officials had reason to expect that the Central Committee would play a larger role. Although Deng Xiaoping's authority as preeminent leader derived not from any formal institutional role but from his personal following and stature, Deng advocated the regularization of party decisionmaking.[10] The potential successors to Deng, such as Hu Yaobang, Zhao Ziyang, Li Peng, and Jiang Zemin, continued to consult regularly with the party elders and behave deferentially to them, but they bet their futures on a broader constituency within the Central Committee by actively promoting reform policies welcomed by the local officials and industrial ministry officials within the Central Committee. Competition for leadership created an opening for policy innovation as contenders tried to construct coalitions within the Central Committee. The decentralizing direction and particularistic form of reform policies were political strategies premised on the influence of the Central Committee, where the largest bloc of members consisted of provincial and municipal officials.

The mandate of the Central Committee to select party leaders and the presence in the Central Committee of party and government officials originally appointed by party leaders create a pattern of authority distinctive to authoritarian regimes that I call "recip-

9. The formal decision to appoint Zhao Ziyang as Hu's replacement was taken by the Thirteenth CCP Congress held ten months later.

10. He served as chairman of the CCP Central Advisory Commission (which has no formal authority) until 1985, on the Standing Committee of the Politburo until 1987, and as head of the CCP Central Military Commission until 1989.

rocal accountability": government officials are accountable to the party leaders who hire and promote them, but party leaders are also accountable to the government officials in the Central Committee selectorate who choose them. Although top-down power is greater than bottom-up power, power flows in both directions.[11] Government officials are both the agents and the constituents of party leaders.

In a period of competition for succession, the political dependence of party leaders on the selectorate becomes more prevalent, and the ability of members of the selectorate to extract resources is enhanced. When the leadership is unified, government officials act in their agent role; they simply ratify the leaders' decisions. But when leaders are actively competing and campaigning for the support of officials in the selectorate—as was the case during the Chinese post-1978 reforms—the influence of second-tier officials on the policy process is more pronounced. Carrying out economic reforms during a period of leadership succession gave the Chinese reforms a distinctive character: contending leaders used reform policies to extend new powers and resources to various groups within the selectorate, and leaders adopted particularistic rather than universal forms of policies, which enabled them to claim credit for giving special treatment to particular organizations and localities.

The Policy Process: Delegation by Consensus

The Chinese government makes policy according to a tacit rule I call "delegation by consensus."[12] The CCP delegates to the State Council the authority to make specific economic decisions. The State Council leaders at the top of the government hierarchy delegate to their subordinates the authority to make decisions if the agents can agree. If the agents reach consensus, the decision is automatically ratified by the higher level; if the agents cannot agree, then the authorities step in to make the decision, or the matter is dropped or tabled until consensus can be achieved.

11. For the reasons top-down power is greater, see Shirk (1993, p. 84).
12. Management specialists call this "management by exception." Lawler (1976).

Delegation by consensus is practiced at each level of the organizational hierarchy: State Council to commissions, commissions to ministries and provinces, and ministries and provinces to bureaus and cities.

Delegation of consensually exercised power is so widespread in hierarchical settings that it could be called the bureaucratic method. From the standpoint of principals, delegation by consensus exploits the superior information of these agents and relieves the principals of the costs of constant intervention in the policy process. Delegation by consensus gives a signal to leaders when one of their core groups is not satisfied. The process of building consensus also provides information about each group's price of support for the policy, which determines whether it will be possible to meet the sum of these prices through compromise and side payments (offers of additional bureaucratic or financial benefits to an agency in exchange for its support of the policies).

From the standpoint of the principal, delegation by consensus works well when it allows key groups to articulate their interests but creates incentives for them to compromise their differences without forcing the principal to intervene. By this standard, Chinese delegation by consensus has not worked well during the 1980s and 1990s. Chen Junsheng, the secretary general of the State Council in 1987, complained that the work of the government had been impeded by constant arguing and "the escalation of coordination" (*xietiao*). Problems that once were resolved at lower levels were pushed up to the State Council or higher. Policymaking had become "a process of repeated negotiation, in which all parties concerned may argue, each holding its ground."[13]

The economic reform agenda, involving a redistribution of authority and rewards among sectors, regions, and bureaucracies, presented a serious political challenge to consensus decisionmaking, which ordinarily produces only incremental change because drastic shifts in the allocation of resources are inhibited by the

13. Chen Junsheng, "Increase the Work Efficiency of Public Organs," *People's Daily*, March 19, 1987, p. 5, in Foreign Broadcast Information Service, *Daily Report: China*, April 1, 1987, pp. K33–34. (Hereafter FBIS, *China*.)

requirement that all agencies agree to them.[14] In China the normative expression of consensus decisionmaking was an ideology one might call "balancism" (*pinghengzhuyi*). According to this ideology, the function of the state is to balance inequities created by arbitrary policies, especially administratively set prices. Fairness requires that no unit lose too much because administrative prices make them less profitable than other units or because the legacies of past government decisions, such as investments in fixed assets, work against them under current formulas. Government bodies are expected to adjust policies to prevent large disparities in benefits among units and prevent some unit from suffering through no fault of its own. Deliberating economic reform policies through a set of institutions operating by consensus and pervaded by balancism was an extremely slow process. A small minority of ministries or provinces that preferred the status quo to the proposed changes could obstruct progress.

Another reason delegation by consensus worked poorly during the reform era was that, particularly in a system of reciprocal accountability, divisions within the party leadership encourage intransigence among government officials. When the party leadership was unified and committed to a policy, it was easy for it to win bureaucratic consensus on the policy. However, competition for succession among party leaders increased uncertainty for government officials and led them to expect solicitous treatment at higher levels. Thinking more like the constituents of top leaders than as their agents, officials dared to block consensus and gamble on a higher-level resolution of the issue.

For most of the 1980s and the 1990s, government bureaucrats perceived CCP leaders as contending for power. By 1981–82 the conflicts between the two most influential elders, Deng Xiaoping and Chen Yun, were readily apparent. Party general secretary Hu

---

14. Vice Premier Tian Jiyun observed in 1986, "The overall reform of the economic structure is, in a sense, a readjustment of power and interest, in which a large amount of contradictions exist. Among them, there are contradictions between the central authorities and the localities; between the state, the collective, and the individual; between one department and another; between one locality and another; between departments and localities; and so on." Tian Jiyun, "Speech at a Conference of Central Organs," Xinhua News Agency, January 11, 1986, in FBIS, *China*, January 13, 1986, p. K5.

Yaobang and Premier Zhao Ziyang, although allies in the drive for economic reform, were competing to succeed Deng Xiaoping and differed over some reform policies. After elderly party conservatives pressured Deng to fire Hu Yaobang in January 1987, it was obvious that party elites were divided by even more fundamental disagreements over the direction of reform. Zhao Ziyang, promoted to party general secretary, was at loggerheads with Li Peng, the newly appointed, more conservative premier. Zhao reportedly complained to Deng, "If there are two different views at the higher level, it is impossible to act in unison at the lower level."[15] After the 1989 Tiananmen protests when Zhao Ziyang lost the power struggle and was fired, the top leadership remained divided between Premier Li Peng and his more reform-minded senior vice premier, Zhu Rongji, with CCP general secretary Jiang Zemin trying to straddle the middle. Reading the signs from Zhongnanhai (the compound where party and government leading organs are housed), many government bureaucrats figured that their chances of winning favorable treatment in a policy package would be enhanced by refusing to compromise and kicking the decision up to the higher level. With the difficulties of achieving bureaucratic consensus aggravated during a period of leadership succession, the approval of any new policy required ample side payments to buy out those who stood to lose by it.

The Chinese Version of Communist Institutions

Why did China succeed in carrying out economic reform without political reform, while the Soviet Union was unable to do so? My explanation focuses on the differences between the Chinese and Soviet communist institutions. Although the two political systems were structurally similar, the Chinese version of communism—less centralized and less well institutionalized—proved to be more flexible than the Soviet one.

Unlike the Soviet Union, where planners in Moscow issued orders to factories throughout the country, the Chinese version of

15. Lo Ping, "Notes on a Northern Journey," *Cheng Ming* (Hong Kong), July 1, 1987, in FBIS, *China*, July 2, 1987, p. K10.

the command economy since the 1950s has been a multitiered, regionally based system in which local governments planned and coordinated much of economic activity.[16] As of 1978 only 50–55 percent of gross industrial output was covered by the central plan; in 1980 only 3 percent of state-owned factories were directly administered by central government ministries.[17] As two prominent Chinese economists wrote, "Strict centralized management of the economy by directives, as under the pure Soviet model, has never existed in China. The 'decentralizing movement' which took place in 1958 and has been renewed from time to time ever since has eroded central planning and its power to control."[18]

The more decentralized character of Chinese economic and financial administration was a legacy of the Maoist era. In two mass campaigns, the Great Leap Forward (1958) and the Cultural Revolution (1966–69), Mao Zedong sought to accelerate economic growth and social transformation over the objections of status quo–oriented central bureaucrats. A key strategy of Mao's was "playing to the provinces," using provincial officials as a political counterweight to the center. Mao appealed to the provincial officials by extending decentralization policies to them and amplified their voice by expanding their representation in the Central Committee.[19] During each of the campaigns, the fiscal system and industrial management and planning system were decentralized to give provincial officials more resources and control. During the Cultural Revolution, the functioning of the central government and party was severely disrupted by the sending down of Beijing officials to the countryside to reform their political attitudes through manual work. In the aftermath of the campaigns, both of which were ultimately viewed as failures, Beijing took back some but not all of the revenues and power it had lost. The consequence of these waves of decentralization was a system in which local governments played a substantially more active eco-

16. Qian Yingyi and Xu Chenggang (1993) have argued that the greater degree of decentralization in China's economic administration than in the Soviet one meant that it was easier to introduce local reforms without risking negative spillover effects to the entire country.

17. Wong (1986).

18. Wu and Zhao (1987, p. 310).

19. Shirk (1993, chap. 9); Chang (1990, pp. 181–89).

nomic role and the center was much weaker than their counterparts in the Soviet Union.

During the Maoist era, waves of administrative decentralization in China had created the possibility that provincial officials could be used as a reformist counterweight to the more conservative center. Although provincial leaders are appointed by the central Communist Party organization, under reciprocal accountability they have the leverage of a key constituency. Individual provinces have many different policy preferences, and the communist prohibition on forming overt factions inhibits provincial officials from coordinating their positions as an organized bloc. Nevertheless, a leader could put provincial officials in his camp by offering them policies that are attractive to all provincial officials, such as reforms enhancing their financial autonomy and resources, and by making special deals for individual provincial officials. Inspired by Mao's historical example, yet guided by a very different policy vision, Deng Xiaoping promoted market reform by playing to the provinces in this way, a possibility that was not available to Gorbachev. Under Deng's direction, local officials became the largest bloc in the Central Committee during the reform era, and a radical decentralization of the fiscal system was implemented early in the reform drive in 1980.[20]

China was not only more decentralized, it also was far behind the Soviet Union in giving institutions, not personalities, the au-

20. Detailed analysis of the Eleventh (1977), Twelfth (1982), Thirteenth (1987), and Fourteenth (1992) Central Committees using consistent standards for coding local officials has not yet been done. Preliminary analyses, however, indicate that the proportion of local officials was increased during periods of reform initiatives and that provincial party secretaries were by far the largest bloc in the Eleventh and Thirteenth Central Committees. During periods when senior conservative leaders were trying to slow down reforms, however, the size of the local group was reduced somewhat and the size of the central group increased; this was the case in the Twelfth and Fourteenth Central Committees. "Paper Analyzes New Central Committee," *South China Morning Post Saturday Review,* November 7, 1987, p. 1, in FBIS, *China,* November 9, 1987, p. 19, on the Twelfth and Thirteenth; Burns (forthcoming), on the Fourteenth. Even in the Twelfth Central Committee, however, when the central government and party officials were increased in number, the provincial party secretaries and governors represented the single largest group. Wang (1992, p. 169). And as Parris Chang points out (1990, p. 233), since many of the military representatives also are based in the provinces, the actual size of the local bloc is larger than it appears from most statistics. Therefore, it is fair to say that during the entire period of reform, local officials constituted the largest bloc in the Central Committee.

thority to make decisions. China was a newer and less well established communist system. Its evolution from personalized rule to institutionalized authority was retarded by Mao Zedong's use of mass campaigns to prevent the routinization of the revolution. As was noted earlier, the authority of the Soviet Central Committee to choose party leaders was definitively established in 1957, while in China the Central Committee still has to share power with party elders who do not even hold official posts. The locus of authority is ambiguous because it is gradually shifting from an informal group of revolutionary elders to the collective institutions of the CCP.

The weakly institutionalized character of CCP institutions proved to be an advantage to Deng Xiaoping and his reformist allies in introducing economic reforms that challenged the vested interests of communist officials in the command economy. In contrast to the Soviet Union, where the dominant leader was constrained by the norms of collective leadership within the party, Deng Xiaoping had the latitude to reshape the membership of the Central Committee and dispense patronage to build support for himself and the reforms. Deng could capitalize on his informal authority (as a Long March elder who had twice been purged by Mao) and his extensive network of clients whom he had placed in influential positions to push reforms forward. In January 1992, when he no longer held any formal post at all, Deng was able to singlehandedly reinvigorate the reform drive after a period of conservative resistance by making a series of speeches on a trip through Southern China. Because of the pluralistic nature of the Chinese economic policy process, Deng would not impose a specific reform policy on the government bureaucracy, but by signaling his general support for market competition and an open economy, he tilted the policy process in that direction.

The more decentralized and less institutionalized character of the Chinese system before reform gave Deng Xiaoping possibilities that Gorbachev lacked. By playing to the provinces and exploiting his personal influence, Deng was able to introduce economic reforms while preserving Communist Party rule. Gorbachev was thwarted by the powerful Soviet central bureaucracy and checked by other party leaders. He had no choice but to shift authority from party to government, create a real legislature, and open the political process to ordinary citizens. These moves eventually produced the fall of the party and the disintegration of the country.

Chapter 4

Patterns in Reform Policies

*T*HIS book is not intended as a comprehensive description of all the changes in China's foreign trade and investment policies since 1978 or of the economic consequences of the changes. What I offer instead is a focused analysis of the way Chinese political institutions shaped these policy changes. Every reform policy had to be channeled through existing communist authoritarian bureaucratic institutions, which proved to be remarkably flexible but left a distinctive mark on policy outputs. After emerging from these institutions, domestic and foreign economic reforms exhibited several consistent features, namely, gradualism, administrative decentralization, and particularistic contracting.

Gradualism

Instead of rushing ahead with a comprehensive, radical transformation of the entire system that would threaten the vested interests of many groups, the reformist leaders were very cautious, as if they were "wading across a river on rocks."[1] Well aware of the political risks of challenging central planners, trade and finance officials, and industrial bureaucrats head-on, the reformers allowed them to retain many of their powers, while encircling them

1. "Reforms Must Be Carried Out Step by Step," *Workers' Daily*, March 13, 1985, p. 1, in Foreign Broadcast Information Service, *Daily Report: China*, March 25, 1985, p. K26. (Hereafter FBIS, *China*.)

27

with new forms of business such as private, collective, and joint venture firms and special economic zones (SEZs). The market sector was expanded gradually while the plan sector was retained. A small zone of market activity began in 1979, when state-owned firms were permitted to sell their above-quota output on their own at market prices and new nonstate firms were allowed to form. The higher prices of the market were a powerful incentive for managers to enter the plan and then to press for smaller plan quotas and more market opportunities. Similarly, although at first few firms were permitted to export, the introduction of the reform allowing these firms to retain a small amount of the foreign exchange they earned created an incentive for all firms to demand more export rights and a larger share of the foreign exchange earnings. Managers and central officials were protected by the security of the old system—the government continued to bail out enterprises operating in the red and restrict the entry of foreign goods to the domestic market—while they gained access to the profitable opportunities of the market at home and abroad. Stimulated by these new incentives, the economy grew rapidly, mainly in the market sector, and economic actors became progressively less dependent on the plan and more oriented toward the market.[2] This strategy of "letting the economy outgrow the plan" was extremely successful in both political and economic terms, although the transitional two-track economy hindered macroeconomic management of investment cycles and produced serious corruption.[3]

A key element of this gradualist approach to reform was substantial side payments to heavy industry, which otherwise would have used its institutional clout to block change. One example of such a side payment was the special contracts granted in 1985 to

2. Byrd (1987, p. 295) argues that the inherent dynamic tendencies of the two-tier system led to a continual increase in the share of the market over time.

3. The phrase is from Naughton (1986, p. 622). Reform economist Wu Jinglian argues that the protracted transition from command to market economy in China was a major cause of corruption. He estimates that the existence of the dual-track system in commodity prices, foreign exchange, and credit interest rates produced extra costs equal to 20–25 percent of the GNP during 1981–88. Wei Ling, "Interview with Wu Jinglian: It Is Necessary to Pay Attention to Corrupt Practices amid 'Business Fever,'" *Jingjii Ribao*, April 6, 1993, in FBIS, *China*, April 30, 1993, p. 17.

the coal, oil, iron and steel, petrochemical, railroad, and military ministries. The ministries were granted rights to sell their above-quota output on their own at higher prices and promised a certain amount of retained profit and state investment in exchange for supplying the plan with a certain amount of products. Although these contracts violated the spirit of the reforms by tightening ministerial allocations of plan quotas and market rights to subordinate enterprises, they were politically expedient. Another side payment was the authority given to the ministries of machinery and electronics to approve foreign imports; this authority allowed them to protect their domestic market (see below). Perhaps the largest side payment to heavy industry was its continued access to the lion's share of central government investment. Reformist leaders initially tried to promote more balanced economic growth by shifting resources to light industry and agriculture in 1980–81. The blow to heavy industry was so severe and its representatives complained so loudly that its share was restored in 1982. Since that time heavy industry has continued to receive favored treatment by the center, while light industry relies on local and self-funding. China's dramatic increases in exports and domestic growth may derive primarily from labor-intensive light industry and agriculture, but central government capital investment does not reflect this change and still favors heavy industry.

Because of the conservative bias of Chinese policymaking institutions, which work according to delegation by consensus, the gradual introduction of a market alongside the traditional planned economy and the continued use of side payments to heavy industry were the only politically feasible approaches. The powerful planning, trade, finance, and industrial agencies that deliberated the design of reforms would have vetoed anything more drastic.[4] Party leaders could have imposed a radical transformation from above, but only if they were themselves unified behind it, a condition difficult to meet during a period of succession. And even if a quick establishment of an open market economy were ordered

4. Agricultural reform, which had only a minor effect on the finance and industrial ministries, progressed more rapidly and smoothly than reforms of industry. There were strong ideological objections to household farming but few bureaucratic ones. See Shirk (1989).

from the top down, obtaining cooperation in implementation from agencies suddenly stripped of their power and resources would have been difficult.

Administrative Decentralization

In an effort to play to the provinces, all reform policies were designed to enhance the resources and economic control of local governments. The 1980 fiscal decentralization was an extremely successful measure to win provincial support for the reform drive. Once local authorities were given an incentive to expand their revenue base by developing local industry, they supported other reforms that would contribute to local industrial development. By making provincial officials the largest bloc in the Central Committee, reformist leaders amplified the influence of this pro-reform group and guaranteed that no ambitious leader in Beijing would risk alienating them. To make sure that provinces were empowered to participate in reform policymaking—despite their lack of a permanent institutional voice in the national government—party leaders decided many policies in work conferences at which provinces as well as ministries were represented.

The consequence of these early moves was that every subsequent reform was framed in such a way as to delegate central economic authority not to enterprises, but to local governments. Reform economists might have envisioned genuine liberalization of industrial management and foreign trade, but, time after time, when the policies emerged from work conferences, the authority and resources intended to go to firm managers had been appropriated by local government officials (and to a lesser degree by ministry officials.)[5] As a senior foreign trade official observed, "Decentralization in foreign trade generally means expansion of decision-making power for the local or departmental administra-

5. As reform economist Zhou Xiaochuan wrote, "Once the central government decides to delegate power to the enterprise, such power may actually fall into the hands of local administrative departments." Zhou Xiaochuan, "Foreign Trade Reform Must Be Coordinated with Other Reforms," *Intertrade*, no. 2 (February 1988), pp. 12–18, in Joint Publication Research Service, *CAR* 88-035, July 1, 1988, p. 18. (Hereafter JPRS.)

tive units, or the shift of power among the administrative departments without touching on the crucial issues of decision-making power for the foreign trade enterprises and the production enterprises. These enterprises are still subjected to departmental and regional administrative restrictions."[6]

The reforms decentralized to local governments the authority to approve foreign investment projects, special trade and investment zones, tax rates for foreign investment firms, establishment of trading companies, export subsidies, allocations of foreign exchange at official rates, and access to the foreign exchange swap markets, along with extensive authority over the domestic economy. Most of the foreign exchange earnings that the center allowed to be retained at the local level were claimed by local governments, not enterprises.

Central planning and trade officials frequently complained that so much power had been decentralized that they were unable to get local officials to obey their orders. Under the reforms, local officials had strong incentives to earn domestic and foreign exchange revenues by attracting foreign investors and expanding industry; they also had individual incentives to extract payoffs from their approval authority. No wonder they turned a deaf ear when Beijing told them, during periods of economic overheating, to stop approving new foreign trade or investment zones or new trading companies. Because provincial officials are still appointed by the central Communist Party leaders, the center could have obtained compliance with its directives if it had tried harder. Under reciprocal accountability, however, it was counter to the interests of central leaders to antagonize the provincial officials, who were such a significant bloc in the Central Committee selectorate. Therefore, central leaders generally refused to back up the efforts of central planning and trade officials to crack down on local actions.[7]

6. Zheng Tuobing, vice minister of foreign economic relations and trade, in Tong Weiming, "Some Views on Industry-Foreign Trade Combination," *Intertrade*, no. 3 (March 1985), pp. 48–49, in JPRS, *China Economic Affairs*, 85-055, June 24, 1985, p. 90.

7. Shirk (1993, pp. 190–96) elaborates this argument that the central leaders have not lost control over local economic behavior, but rather that they choose not to enforce their control.

Particularistic Contracting

A striking feature of Chinese domestic and foreign economic reforms was the prevalence of what I call "particularistic contracting." Instead of standardized rules to be applied uniformly to all units (including provincial and local governments, ministries, and enterprises) reforms were designed as ad hoc arrangements to be negotiated by government for each individual unit or set of units. This selectivism of reform policies, which translated into patronage opportunities, suited the incentives of communist leaders who were competing for the support of subordinate officials. Particularistic contracting was successful in the context of communist political institutions because it mimicked the familiar pattern by which production, supply, and trade quotas were bargained out and political support networks built under traditional central planning. Particularistic contracting perpetuated the patrimonial style of Chinese communist politics and exploited it to generate political support for reforms.

Particularistic contracting can be identified in all fiscal, industrial, and foreign trade and investment reforms introduced since 1978: the fiscal contracts between the center and the provinces; the profit contracting system for enterprises; the SEZs, fourteen open cities, and innumerable technology development zones; foreign trade contracts between the center and the provinces; foreign exchange retention contracts between the center and the provinces; and access to the foreign exchange swap market.

First, a program offering special treatment, usually involving access to higher-priced markets, was initiated as an experiment in a small number of provinces, cities, ministries, or enterprises. The label *experiment* is a misnomer, because they were designed not to test the results of a policy change but to build bureaucratic support for it. Units chosen to implement experiments were favored with preferential treatment such as low-priced inputs, electricity, and bank loans. No experiment was allowed to fail. Chinese reform experiments bore close resemblance to the model communes and factories promoted as propaganda and patronage devices during Mao Zedong's era.

When other officials perceived the benefits of the experiment, they clamored for it to be extended to their units as well. Leaders were happy to spread the rewards of reform to more grateful clients. Even after reforms were popularized, they continued in particularistic contracting form with specific terms, such as profit, revenue, or foreign exchange retention rates, negotiated for each unit. To put it crudely, officials sold contracts in exchange for bribes or political support.[8] In many instances, central officials shared the proceeds by authorizing the local officials to negotiate particularistic arrangements with lower-level administrative agencies and enterprises.

The particularistic contracting formula created bureaucratic demand for scarce lucrative reform opportunities. How one was treated by the policy was just as valuable as money. Being chosen as a reform experiment or obtaining a generous foreign exchange retention contract could mean a windfall. Officials and managers, uncertain about the future of administrative intervention and lacking legally secure property rights, had no choice but to invest effort in seeking this kind of policy patronage.

The gradualism, administrative decentralization, and particularistic contracting of the Chinese reforms explain why were they were politically successful and sustainable over a fifteen-year period. Communist officials at all levels of the system retained their prior subsidies and protections while gaining new opportunities for personal or political gain.

8. Wei Ling,"Interview with Wu Jinglian."

Chapter 5

Foreign Economic Reform Policies

A T the Third Plenum of the Eleventh Central Committee in December 1978, China embarked on an ambitious program of economic reform aimed at improving economic performance and raising living standards. From the beginning, foreign investment and trade were an integral part of the reform drive. Two of the most significant sets of policies are analyzed below from a political-institutional perspective.

Regional Policies toward Foreign Investment

Foreign direct investment has played a very important role in China's post-1978 economic development. As a very late developer, China was able to take advantage of the expansion of international finance during the 1970s, utilizing foreign capital more than its Asian neighbors who developed earlier, like Japan. And the Chinese living outside the mainland, commonly called the "overseas Chinese," were a huge source of assets that the PRC could tap. Although the December 1978 communiqué initiating the reform drive made no mention of foreign investment, a few days following its publication senior party leader Li Xiannian announced that China would begin to welcome foreign investment.

Special Economic Zones

Six months later the joint venture law and the creation of the special economic zones (SEZs) were formally approved. Four zones were established: three in Guangdong Province—Shenzhen (the best known), Zhuhai, and Shantou—and one in Fujian Province (Xiamen). The objective of the SEZ policy was to attract foreign investment by offering concessionary terms and a good business climate. Like the export-processing zones established in Korea, Taiwan, and other developing countries in the 1960s and 1970s, most of the industry in the SEZs was expected to process imported materials for export.

Anticipating the most likely early investors to be overseas Chinese, policymakers located the zones in South China, which was near Hong Kong, Taiwan, and Singapore and was the original home of many overseas Chinese. The hope was that although international corporations might be wary of the economic and political risks of investing in the PRC, any caution on the part of overseas Chinese businesspeople would be swept away by their eagerness to express their patriotism and create jobs for their kinsmen by setting up new factories in China. The enthusiasm of the overseas Chinese for doing business on the mainland has proved to be an extremely valuable ingredient in China's economic success. Since the reform drive began, approximately 90 percent of China's foreign investment has come from overseas Chinese, mostly from Hong Kong and Taiwan. Overseas Chinese businesspeople also have been an important source of business expertise and marketing connections.

While it was obviously sensible to attract overseas Chinese capital by opening Southern China to foreign investment, what was the logic of permitting only four zones? There were two reasons for establishing such a small number of sites.

First, starting out with only a few zones prevented the new policies toward foreign investment from being blocked by opposition from Communist Party and government officials.[1] After thirty years of almost complete isolation from the world economy, many Chinese leaders remained committed to the notion of national self-reliance. Taking their cues from Mao's perspective, they argued that China's experience with nineteenth-century Western imperialism proved that economic intercourse led to foreign dom-

1. Crane (1990, pp. 28–29).

ination and cultural pollution. Deng Xiaoping had become the target of this kind of xenophobic backlash when he suggested in the mid-1970s that expanding foreign trade would strengthen China as a nation; his position was condemned as characteristic of "lackeys and compradors in the service of foreign bosses."[2] When new foreign trade and investment reforms were introduced in the late 1970s, strong cultural and ideological objections were heard from the inland provinces and heavy industries that had been favored and protected by the policy of autarky.[3] The establishment of four special zones could be presented to conservative skeptics as a way to gain the benefits of foreign investment while restricting foreign cultural influence to only a few small areas, much like the trading ports of the Ming dynasty, the treaty ports of the Qing dynasty, and the extraterritorial concessions of the late Qing and early Republican periods.[4]

The creation of the special economic zones was a way to reduce resistance to the new open policies from the powerful planning, finance, and industrial bureaucracies. Instead of forcing the central bureaucracies to change the way they planned and administered the economy, the pro-reform leaders bypassed them by exempting the SEZs from the strictures of the command economy. The zones were given unique freedoms to organize their economies on a market basis with floating prices.[5] Their experiments with labor markets, open bidding for construction contracts, and other market-style innovations put them at the vanguard of the domestic reform process.[6] A separate SEZ office was established under the State Council not to manage the zones, but to run interference for them with the central bureaucracies. When first created, the SEZs and their office in Beijing had a very difficult time obtaining the

2. Zheng (1985).

3. Shirk (1984); *A Summary Chronology of Major Events* (1987, p. 449); Crane (1990, p. 36).

4. Harding (1987, p. 163); Yang (1991a, p. 44).

5. Zhou Bingteng, "Price Reform in Shenzhen Provides a Lesson in Successful Reform," *Social Science*, no. 8 (August 1985, pp. 22–24), in Joint Publications Research Service, *China Economic Affairs*, 85-105, November 27, 1985, pp. 77–83. (Hereafter JPRS.)

6. The extent of economic transformation in Guangdong is reflected in the fact that in 1993 only 7.6 percent of Guangdong enterprises were still owned by the state. Guangdong People's Radio Network, June 8, 1993, in Foreign Broadcast Information Service, *Daily Report: China*, June 14, 1993, p. 65. (Hereafter FBIS, *China.*)

materials, labor, and capital they needed for their development. In the late 1970s and early 1980s, national and local plans still claimed almost all resources, leaving slim pickings for the SEZ enterprises (along with private and collective firms in other places) that were operating outside the plan. Over time, however, as the market sector expanded, it became easier for SEZ enterprises to obtain needed inputs.

The second reason for limiting special zone status to only four locations was that it allowed Deng Xiaoping and other communist leaders to exploit the political advantages of particularism. Extending special privileges to particular localities earned leaders political credit with the provincial authorities in Guangdong and Fujian. Although Deng Xiaoping may not have originated the SEZ policy, he soon became personally associated with it.[7] As a native of South China, he must have been pleased to liberate this region from the heavy-handed redistributive control of the center that had retarded its development in the Maoist era.

The policies extended to the four zones and to Guangdong and Fujian provinces involved more than the freedom to offer concessionary tax policies to foreign investors and to escape the plan. Beijing also blessed these areas with generous financial subsidies in the form of fiscal and foreign exchange revenue contracts. Beginning in 1980, Guangdong and Fujian were awarded five-year fiscal contracts permitting them to retain almost all of the taxes and industrial profits generated by firms in their jurisdiction. (Guangdong was obligated to pay the center only 1 billion yuan a year and Fujian received a subsidy from the center of 150 million yuan annually; all other revenues were the provinces' to keep.) In contrast, the three provincial-level cities of Beijing, Shanghai, and Tianjin were still required to turn over from 63 to 88 percent of their revenues.[8] The special financial incentives for Guangdong and Fujian motivated provincial officials to develop their local economies in a pragmatic, profit-oriented manner. Guangdong, in particular, became an economic success story and was able to reduce its dependence on central infrastructure and capital invest-

7. Naughton (1993, p. 509).
8. Oksenberg and Tong (1991).

ment funds from 80 percent of the total in 1979 to 2 percent in 1992.[9]

The foreign exchange retention deals awarded to the SEZs and their home provinces were also unusually generous. The SEZs were allowed to retain all of the hard currency they earned from trade, in contrast with the average of 25 percent allowed other localities. Guangdong and Fujian also were granted special foreign exchange retention rates higher than those for other provinces.

Geographic particularism proved to be a potent strategy for reorienting local officials away from self-reliance and toward the world economy. Envy has a powerful effect on policy preferences. When officials from other provinces saw the economic benefits Guangdong, Fujian, and the SEZs received from exports, joint ventures, and freedom from the plan, they began to press for the same opportunities. They coveted the color television assembly lines and Japanese automobiles imported by the zones and their provinces. And they knew that they could not compete with the zones and their provinces for foreign business partners or export markets unless they were granted similar discretion over tax rates and other terms. They also wanted the preferential rates of revenue and foreign exchange retention extended to them. By the mid-1980s even the inland provinces, which had begun as fierce opponents of the open policy, were demanding more access to the open door.[10] Geographic competition for particularistic foreign economic benefits produced an open door bandwagon.[11]

Although politically successful, the policy of regional particularism had some negative economic consequences. One significant loss was the slow pace of economic progress in Shanghai, whose economic potential remained shackled by the center's fiscal de-

9. Carl Goldstein, "Full Speed Ahead: Guangdong Party Congress Ignores Calls to Slow Growth," *Far Eastern Economic Review,* June 3, 1993, p. 21.
10. Yang (1991b, p. 57). Not everyone was persuaded that the SEZs were a good idea. In 1985 central planning and industrial officials launched major criticisms of the SEZs for continuing to soak the central treasury for funds and for insufficient exports and technology imports. Deng Xiaoping, apparently impressed by the intensity of the criticisms, appeared to back away from his previously wholehearted support of the zones, now describing them merely as "experiments." Central investment in the zones was also curtailed. See Harding (1987, p. 169).
11. Yang (1991b, p. 57).

mands and administrative controls while the SEZs zoomed ahead. In a 1984 interview with me, the then-mayor of Shanghai, Wang Daohan, complained bitterly about the preferential treatment extended to the SEZs but not to Shanghai. Deng Xiaoping, in a 1992 speech, conceded his mistake: "In retrospect, one of my big errors was the exclusion of Shanghai when the four special economic zones were instituted. Otherwise, the Yangtze Delta, the entire Yangtze Valley and even the whole country would now have presented a different picture as far as reform and opening to the outside world is concerned."[12]

Extending the Open Policy

Pressure from other provinces led the State Council in 1984 to extend freedoms similar to those of the SEZs to Hainan Island and fourteen coastal cities.[13] The move came after what the Chinese press described euphemistically as "heated discussions."[14] The new open cities were permitted to offer tax incentives for foreign investment similar to, but less generous than, those offered in the SEZs. The cities, however, were also encouraged to create technical development zones that could offer terms as generous as those offered in the SEZs (see below). To satisfy local officials in coastal areas that were not chosen as open cities, in 1985 the State Council extended similar treatment to the deltas of the Pearl, Yangtze, and Min Rivers.

In 1988 CCP general secretary Zhao Ziyang broadened the reach of the open policy to the entire coastal zone with its population of over 200 million. Zhao, who was at the time under considerable pressure from party conservatives, sought backing among coastal officials by traveling through many of the coastal provinces and drumming up support for his "coastal development policy."[15]

12. "Importance of Development Stressed," Xinhua News Agency, November 5, 1993 in FBIS, *China,* November 5, 1993, p. 32.
13. The fourteen cities are Dalian, Qinhuangdao, Tianjin, Yantai, Qingdao, Lianyung-ang, Nantong, Shanghai, Ningbo, Wenzhou, Fuzhou, Guangzhou, Zhanjiang, and Beihai.
14. "The Birth of an Important Decision—A New Step in Opening the Country to the World," *Nanfang Ribao,* June 11, 1984, p. 2, in FBIS, *China,* June 18, 1984, p. K1.
15. Yang (1991a, p. 45). According to Yu Yu-lin (1988, p. 3), Zhao's coastal development policy was the subject of a contentious Politburo meeting on May 30 through June 1, 1988.

In this policy, Zhao defended the concept of unbalanced growth by arguing that the economic and cultural differences between the coastal and inland areas made it impossible for all parts of the country to develop at the same speed; therefore the coastal areas should be allowed to move ahead by using their better labor, communications and infrastructure, and scientific and technological capacity to attract foreign business and expand exports.

Appealing to the coastal region as a whole did not mean the end of particularism, however. Zhao's coastal zone strategy was implemented by creating special open zones in eight counties and municipalities. After Zhao was fired in 1989, Premier Li Peng, despite his reputation as a conservative with leanings toward the center, adopted a succession strategy that involved building his own provincial support base. Capitalizing on the resentment Shanghai had long felt toward Guangdong's special privileges, Li Peng became the patron of Shanghai's new Pudong economic development area and granted Shanghai both greater autonomy over foreign trade and investment and more revenues.[16]

Meanwhile, inland provinces were clamoring for their own special trade and investment zones. The central authorities responded to the demand by extending zone-like privileges to small batches of particular areas. In the early 1980s, remote Xinjiang Province and Tibet were granted the same preferential 100 percent foreign exchange retention rate as Guangdong and Fujian, a largely symbolic gesture considering the small quantity of their exports.[17] In 1985, the State Council approved a special 50 percent rate for four autonomous regions—Inner Mongolia, Xinjiang, Guangxi, and Ningxia—and three provinces—Yunnan, Guizhou, and Qinghai—in China's interior.[18] The granting of special rights to particular provinces only fueled the demands from other areas. The 1988 coastal development strategy policy included three localities in inland Sichuan among the eight granted special open zone status.[19]

16. Elizabeth Cheng, "Balancing Act: Shanghai's Pudong Project Gets a Boost," *Far Eastern Economic Review*, March 26, 1992, p. 61. As noted earlier, Deng Xiaoping also advocated the unleashing of Shanghai's economic potential.

17. Lardy (1992b, p. 55).

18. Lardy (1992b, pp. 55–56). Lardy notes that at the time the exports from these eight administrative areas constituted less than 4 percent of China's total exports.

19. Yang (1991a, p. 54).

In June 1992, Beijing authorized twenty-one additional cities, located along the Yangtze River and in the Northeast, to offer special incentives to foreign investors.[20]

One of the most effective measures for spurring inland provinces to engage in international business was the authorization of particular local governments to create special development zones where they were permitted to offer concessionary terms to foreign investors. In essence, this policy was a mechanism for central officials to share with local officials the payoffs generated by particularism. The authority to grant development zone status to a particular suburb or neighborhood was an attractive form of patronage that local officials could extend to subordinates in exchange for political support or other favors. The first beneficiaries of the development zone policy were in coastal cities, but Li Peng subsequently extended the policy to inland areas.[21] The development zone policy was extremely popular among local leaders, who saw it not only as a way to gain access to international business but also "as a means of gaining benefit and privilege."[22] During the first nine months of 1992, almost 2,000 development zones were set up, a large proportion of them in inland areas. As a result, the inland provinces raised their 1992 share of foreign capital attracted to China from 7 percent to 10 percent.[23] By early 1993 the press was reporting that "nobody knows exactly how many such zones, which attract investment with a variety of tax breaks and other favorable policies, have been launched in China."[24]

20. Carl Goldstein, "Numbers Game," *Far Eastern Economic Review*, December 24, 1992, p. 72.

21. Previously, in 1988, some impatient inland officials had established development zones without permission. Yang (1991b, p. 58).

22. Shi Jian," 'Policy Auctions' in Development Zones Viewed," *Zhongguo Tongxun She* (Hong Kong), November 4, 1992, in FBIS, *China*, November 25, 1992, p. 28.

23. Lu Ren, "Jiang Zemin Issues Order on Rectifying Development Zones," *Ching Pao* (Hong Kong), June 5, 1993, pp. 34–35, in FBIS, *China*, June 7, 1993, p. 35; Lu Tong, "Foreign Investors Are Spreading to Central and Western China," China News Agency, May 27, 1993, in FBIS, *China*, June 11, 1993, p. 26.

24. Yin Xin, "Government to Tighten Restrictions on Zones," *China Daily Business Weekly*, February 7, 1993, p. 1, in FBIS, *China*, February 9, 1993, p. 33. According to this source, the State Economic Planning Commission estimates 1,700 zones, the State Council SEZ Office, 1,800, the State Land Administration, 2,700, and the Ministry of Agriculture, 9,000. The first three figures include zones at the national (95), provincial, and city level; the last one includes those at the township level. Even the People's Liberation Army has its own national development zone located in the Shantou SEZ. "PLA Inaugurates Economic Development Zone," Xinhua News Agency, February 12, 1993, in *FBIS*, China, February 12, 1993, p. 17.

The uncontrolled spread of development zones created unintended negative consequences, however, such as economic overheating; shortages of funds, energy, transport, and raw materials; the appropriation of good farmland for factories; and competitive cutting of tax rates and land prices to attract foreign investors. The State Council responded in 1993 by reinstituting the requirement of central approval for all new development zones.[25] CCP General Secretary Jiang Zemin ordered an inspection and rectification of all zones in order to close down those that lacked infrastructure and other conditions to support foreign firms. Premier Li Peng was assigned the job of heading the interministerial central inspection team, not an enviable task for an ambitious central politician who needed to ingratiate himself with provincial officials.[26]

By the early 1990s, the selective authorization of specially privileged open zones, beginning with a small number and gradually adding more, had effectively broadened the support of regional officials for the reform drive. The location of foreign investment projects continued to be highly skewed toward the coastal areas and South China—according to one estimate about 90 percent of the cumulative investments had gone into the coastal provinces and 40 percent to Guangdong alone—but inland provinces were actively seeking investors. A huge surge of investment from Japan and South Korea after 1992, located primarily in the Northeast and in Shandong Province, was very significant in broadening the geography of support for the open policy. Trade and investment flows around the Sea of Japan create a new dynamic natural economic territory that will balance the territory around Taiwan, South China, and Hong Kong.

Although the economic gap between coastal and inland regions may have grown as a result of the open policy, significant benefits did trickle down to inland areas. Inland government organizations and enterprises rushed to get a piece of the action by setting up businesses in the SEZs. With its market economy and access to

25. Governments below the provincial level were stripped of authority to approve development zones, and all approvals by provinces, autonomous regions, and municipalities had to be ratified by the State Council. "State Council Issues Development Zone Circular," Xinhua News Agency, May 15, 1993, in FBIS, *China*, May 18, 1993, p. 43.

26. Lu, "Jiang Zemin Issues Order on Rectifying Development Zones."

foreign funds and markets, Shenzhen became a major domestic trade entrepôt where steel, cars, and consumer goods could be bought and sold (administrative blockades erected by provincial officials had created a tremendous demand for interregional trade). SEZ-based shipping lines were created to transport this entrepôt trade. The inward domestic orientation of the SEZs was viewed as a problem by some who criticized the zones' inadequate levels of exports.[27] Yet the economic ties between the coastal zones and the inland areas created benefits for both and widened the base of political support for the open policy.[28]

The SEZs have lost some of their competitive advantage as the demands from other regions and the objections of GATT to preferential policies have pushed Beijing to move toward a more level playing field throughout China. The zones have resisted this trend vociferously. As a result, they were allowed to delay implementation of some of the higher taxes required by the 1994 national tax law. Zone officials also are ingenious at proposing new forms of preferential treatment to the center. As a Hainan zone official told a journalist, "If our special policies aren't special any more, we'll create some new ones."[29]

The geographic particularism of China's approach to attracting foreign investment was dictated largely by political expediency. Reformist leaders bypassed the opposition of central bureaucracies by creating zones exempt from central planning and control. And national leaders viewed the distribution of special zone status as an excellent source of patronage with which they could win appreciation and support from provincial officials. From an economic perspective, granting preferential treatment to these zones to induce foreign firms to invest in them creates distortions and wasteful rents. Yet the particularistic approach was remarkably

27. Tzeng (1991, pp. 274–75).
28. During 1992–93 large amounts of capital flowed to coastal regions, where it was used to speculate in the real estate and stock markets and helped create a "bubble economy." Yang Liu, "Rebuked by Zhu Rongji for Seeking Private Gains, County and Bank Senior Officials in Hunan Dismissed from Posts," *Ming Pao* (Hong Kong), August 5, 1993, p. 7, in FBIS, *China*, August 6, 1993, p. 25; Lena H. Sun, "China Tries to Keep the Lid on a Boiling Economy," *Washington Post National Weekly Edition*, July 12–18, 1993, p. 16.
29. Karl Huus, "One Province, No System," *Far Eastern Economic Review*, June 2, 1994, p. 47.

successful at reorienting Chinese officials, particularly those from inland areas, toward the world economy and at maintaining national unity despite the fissures and gaps caused by international economic competition.

The Decentralization of Foreign Trade Authority

Under the traditional command economy, China achieved a high degree of economic control but at the price of a low volume of foreign trade. The Ministry of Foreign Trade (later called the Ministry of Foreign Economic Relations and Trade, or MOFERT, and now called the Ministry of Foreign Trade and Economic Cooperation, or MOFTEC) and its handful of foreign trade corporations (FTCs) enforced mandatory import and export plans at administratively set fixed prices completely unrelated to international prices. All foreign exchange was collected and distributed by MOFTEC. Enterprises had no incentive to engage in foreign trade because buying and selling at home was just as rewarding. Because exports and imports were decoupled, exporting did not give an enterprise the right to import (or vice versa). Since the 1970s, implementing the national foreign trade plan had produced domestic currency losses for the central state because subsidization was required to compensate for domestic price distortions. Imports of food grains and chemical fertilizer, purchased at international market prices but sold at low domestic fixed prices, cost the state renminbi (the domestic currency). So did exports of many manufactured goods such as machinery and electronics, purchased at high fixed domestic prices and sold at international market prices. The disparity in domestic and international prices of some products produced domestic currency earnings from trade, but they did not cover the financial losses.

The goals of reforming China's foreign trade administration were to increase the volume of trade, particularly exports, while reducing the government's financial burden from trade. The government could have created a more incentive-compatible system of foreign trade administration by a number of different measures. For example, it could have freed up domestic prices to converge with international prices. Drastic price reform, however, would have redistributed profits and losses among economic sectors (with particularly deleterious effects on powerful manufacturing industries such as machinery) and was infeasible in a system operating by delegation by consensus. The government could also have devolved trading authority down to the firm level and allowed firms to deal directly with foreigners and keep their own hard currency, which could be freely exchanged. Government bureaucrats, however, were not ready to abrogate that degree of economic control.

Local Trade Corporations

The option chosen was more politically practical: decentralization of trade authority from MOFTEC to provinces and ministries but not to firms, combined with particularistic contracts for sharing foreign exchange. It was provincial and ministry officials, not ordinary managers, who were empowered to make policy demands and to whom political leaders were accountable. And by retaining the selective bureaucratically controlled access to foreign exchange instead of putting it on a market basis, officials created ways to reward themselves.[30]

Decentralization meant that provincial and municipal governments as well as ministries were permitted to establish their own trading companies in competition with the MOFTEC ones. The central trade monopoly was demolished. Previously a dozen MOFTEC trading companies managed all foreign trade; under the reforms, the number of FTCs established by ministries, provinces, and cities grew to about 800 in 1986, reached more than 5,000 in 1987, and dropped back to 3,673 as of August 1991.[31] Provincial

30. A small number of large enterprises have been granted the right to trade directly, a valuable status conferred by the provincial trade department. In Jiangsu in 1991, only twenty-seven such enterprises and business groups existed. Panagariya (1991, p. 6.) A 1993 report states that nationwide, 1,360 firms have been given trading rights. Gao Haihao and Wu Xiaobo, "More Enterprises to be Given Foreign Trade Rights," Xinhua News Agency, May 28, 1993, in FBIS, *China*, June 8, 1993, p. 37.

31. Lardy (1992a, p. 702). During 1988–89 the center contracted the number of FTCs by reasserting control over the approval of new ones.

officials traveled the world promoting their local products. Governors commuted to their offices in Toyotas.

The decentralization of trade authority was combined with a system allowing local firms and governments to retain a share of their foreign exchange export earnings, an attempt to provide an incentive to sell abroad by compensating for the domestic-international price gap and the overvalued Chinese currency. Foreign exchange retention rights were assigned on a particularistic basis. These retention rights were essentially import entitlements of tremendous value because of the very overvalued exchange rate. Domestic economic growth generated a great hunger for imports of both manufacturing equipment and consumer goods; the disparities between domestic and international prices made manufactured imports a bargain; and years of economic isolation had created a pent-up demand for imports. In this environment, foreign exchange retention rights were a valuable selective benefit that officials could distribute to their friends and supporters or keep for themselves. Reflecting the plurality of provincial leaders in the selectorate, the foreign exchange retention system was tilted toward the provinces, which were initially allowed to keep 40 percent of earnings above the base level, and away from central ministries, which were allowed only 20 percent. As a result of this system, the percentage of foreign exchange in the hands of provinces and export producers increased from essentially zero before 1979 to 42 percent in the mid-1980s.[32]

Over the 1980s, the authority to regulate foreign investment was also transferred to provincial and local authorities and generated additional opportunities for them to benefit.[33] Some of these rewards came in the form of free trips abroad, foreign scholarships for children, or other gifts from foreign firms that sought approval for a new joint venture or access for an existing joint venture to

32. Lardy (1992b, pp. 53, 57). As a general rule, half the retained hard currency was given to the enterprise and half to the level of government that managed the enterprise.

33. Provincial governments, in turn, can delegate to lower-level governments authority to approve and regulate joint ventures and the opportunity to collect rewards. See Liu Lei, "Beijing Delegates the Authority to Examine and Approve Foreign-Funded Enterprise Contracts and Articles of Association to Lower Levels," *Guoji Shangbao*, November 7, 1988, p. 1, in JPRS, *CAR*, January 19, 1989, pp. 48–49.

some form of preferential treatment.[34] A policy like the October 1986 provisions for the encouragement of foreign investment, which granted the right to sell on the domestic market and convert renminbi earnings to foreign exchange (along with other privileges) to export-oriented and technologically advanced joint ventures, was a good example of such preferential treatment. The policy delegated the authority to interpret the flexible guidelines for establishing whether a joint venture qualified for these categories to provincial and local authorities (who were to reevaluate these qualifications annually).[35] Competition with other localities for foreign investment, as earlier noted, gave local officials an incentive to collude with foreign business in cutting or evading taxes. National tax policies that discriminate in favor of joint ventures tempted local firms to become a fake joint venture by creating a dummy company in Hong Kong, a practice that involved the complicity of local officials who serve as Beijing's tax collectors.[36]

Decentralization also entailed shifting the authority to issue import and export licenses from central to local officials while expanding the number of products requiring licenses. According to a study of Guangdong Province, "87 products required export licenses in 1985, 127 in 1986, 217 in 1987, and 257 in 1988." Of these 257 products, 35 were issued licenses by MOFTEC, 56 by special agencies of MOFTEC, and 166 by provincial Economic and Trading Commissions.[37] Each approval was an opportunity for an offical to claim a favor in return.

34. "Foreign trade is a choice cut of meat. Those involved not only can make money and acquire goods; they can also go abroad." Shao Wei-chia, "New Foreign Trade 'Reform Plane,' " *Economic Reporter* (Hong Kong), October 1, 1990, in JPRS, *CAR,* November 28, 1990, p. 38.

35. The *China Business Review* advised foreign investors that "since local officials—usually in the foreign economic relations and trade departments—issue the certifications, decisions may be subject to the priorities and whims of each locale." It reports that the certification of export-oriented ventures is based on objective statistical criteria, but the certification of technologically advanced ventures is more subjective. Potter (1988, pp. 36–37). For central regulations intended to clarify the ambiguity of the two categories, see *Guoji Shangbao,* February 15, 1992, in JPRS, *CAR,* July 13, 1992, pp. 7–9.

36. Wang Yong, "State Orders Crackdown on Tax Loopholes," *China Daily,* August 6, 1993, in FBIS, *China,* August 6, 1993, p. 28; Dai Zigeng, "What We Should Say about 'False Joint Ventures,' " *Guangming Daily,* April 4, 1993, in FBIS, *China,* May 4, 1993, pp. 30–31. The latter source contains interesting quotes reflecting the opposite views on this phenomenon from local big enterprises and a Guangdong provincial official.

37. Zhang and Zou (1994, p. 170).

The new decentralized trade regime established in 1979 proved to perpetuate the system's traditional bias toward imports and against exports, even with the new export incentives. Because of the international-domestic price differential, reselling imported manufactured goods on the domestic market was an extremely profitable business for local FTCs, and exporting manufactured goods was usually not profitable. The amount of foreign exchange a company could earn depended on its volume of exports, not the profitability of its operations. Because the central treasury continued to subsidize all FTC domestic currency losses from exports, it made sense for local officials to export regardless of the size of their losses. And, as Shan Weijian notes, because lower export prices meant increased export sales, the local authorities' profitability was positively correlated to the losses incurred in exporting.[38] The financial burden of underwriting the losses generated by FTC trading activities weighed heavily on the central state: in 1986 direct fiscal subsidies to foreign trade companies to cover their losses amounted to over 24 billion yuan, an amount greater than 2 percent of China's GNP and the official budget deficit.[39] A secondary negative effect of decentralization combined with foreign exchange retention was that FTCs bought up cheaply priced agricultural produce for export, driving up the domestic price and wreaking havoc on the national plan.[40]

One consequence of trade decentralization that Beijing officials found particularly galling was the loss of national bargaining power with foreigners. Voices from the center asked plaintively, "After

38. Shan (1989, pp. 37–38).
39. World Bank (1994, p. 26). For Chinese perspectives on the problem of foreign trade financial losses, see Zhou Jianping and Zhao Kaitai, "Views on Solving the Problem of Current Foreign Trade Losses," *Finance, Trade, and Economics*, no. 1 (January 1993), pp. 45–48, in JPRS, *China Economic Affairs*, 83-504, pp. 62–69; Li Gonghao, "A Preliminary Study of the Problems of Pricing Import and Export Commodities," *World Economic Forum*, no. 1 (February 20, 1983), pp. 37–42, in JPRS, *China Economic Affairs*, 84-013, pp. 28–39. Zhang Amei and Zou Gang note that countries like India, Pakistan, Kenya, and China experience "trade-off-deficits": "The higher the fiscal deficit, the lower the trade deficit, and vice versa, as a result of fiscal subsidies supporting foreign trade." Zhang and Zou (1994, p. 156).
40. Li, "A Preliminary Study of the Problems of Pricing Import and Export Commodities," p. 35; Zhou Xiaochuan, "Foreign Trade Reform Must Be Coordinated with Other Reforms," *Intertrade*, no. 2 (February 1988), pp. 12–18, in JPRS, *CAR*, 88-035, p. 15.

the expansion of the localities' power of management during the restructuring, why should there be competition among ourselves resulting in benefits for foreigners?"[41] The two-track currency and price systems were partially responsible for the price gouging and tax and land giveaways by which local authorities competed for export markets and foreign investment; yet even in a more thoroughly marketized economic environment, the decentralization of trade authority and the interregional competition it produces inevitably weaken the leverage of the nation as a whole vis-à-vis foreign firms.[42] Not surprisingly, the solution proposed in Beijing for the problem was the "elimination of overlapping operations" by restoring the central foreign trade monopoly.[43]

The problems caused by trade reforms, summed up at the time as "raising procurement prices at home, slashing prices abroad, letting an outflow of profits," sparked a major policy debate during 1982–83.[44] The central authorities succeeded in imposing an extensive import and export licensing system, but not in reinstituting the central trade monopoly. The market-oriented economists and local officials relied on a more market-conforming approach to the problem of high renminbi costs of export earnings, that is, the dual exchange rates created in 1981. An internal settlement rate was set at 2.80 yuan to $1 U.S., against the official exchange rate of 1.53. In conjunction with a cutback of domestic construction projects, the more depreciated secondary exchange rate helped reduce imports and increase exports. China ran a trade surplus in 1981, 1982, and 1983.

Another round of decentralization in 1984–85, spurred by the big push in domestic industrial reform, freed FTCs, even those administered by MOFTEC, from central government administration and allowed firms to select an FTC to act as their representative in import and export business and pay them by commission. This new "agency system" was supposed to make FTCs more businesslike and require producing firms and FTCs to be respon-

41. Zhu Naixiao, "Effective Ways to Restructure Our Foreign Trade System Explored," *Inquiry into Economic Problems*, no. 7 (July 1984), pp. 7–10, in JPRS, *China Economic Affairs*, 84-105, p. 76.
42. Shirk (1990).
43. Zhu, "Effective Ways to Restructure Our Foreign Trade System Explored," p. 77.
44. Zhou, "Foreign Trade Reform Must Be Coordinated with Other Reforms."

sible for their own losses.[45] At the same time the agency system was introduced, foreign exchange retention ratios were raised, and exports above the plan level became subject to a preferential retention rate.[46] During interviews at the time, Beijing officials acknowledged that the agency system had no teeth to force financial discipline on FTCs and firms. The central state would still have to bail out firms with trade losses. FTCs ignored the agency policy when it came to exports, preferring to continue to purchase goods from the factory and sell them on their own account because that was the only way they could have a claim on foreign exchange retention. The enhanced foreign exchange retention ratios designed to promote exports, however, were inadequate, given the continued overvaluation of the renminbi. In fact, the surge in domestic demand triggered by the loosening of controls over the domestic economy and foreign trade in 1984 produced a much larger flow of imports (particularly consumer durables), a trade deficit, and a hemorrhage of foreign exchange reserves that began at the end of 1984 and worsened in 1985.

An additional negative consequence of the decentralized trade regime was an increase in bureaucratic corruption, which became a major issue in 1984–85. Much of the behavior labeled corruption in China would be considered legitimate business in other countries: it exploits government-created preferential treatment to earn profits often pocketed by organizations, not by individuals. The most notorious case of trade-related corruption in China, the 1985 Hainan Island automobile import scandal, is a good example. Hainan officials took advantage of the authority granted them as an open zone to arrange the locality's own imports. The officials imported automobiles and resold them at a huge profit in Guangdong and other provinces that were not allowed to import vehicles. They then converted their renminbi earnings into hard currency that they used to finance the import of more cars. When the

45. Zhong Yi, "Be a Good Agent to Render All-Round Service," *Intertrade*, no. 3 (March 1985), pp. 42–43, in JPRS, *China Economic Affairs*, 85-055, June 24, 1985, pp. 88–89; Ji Chongwei, "New Expectations and Hope for Our Foreign Trade," *Outlook*, March 4, 1985, p. 27, in JPRS, *China Economic Affairs*, 85-054, June 18, 1985, pp. 66–68.

46. Lardy (1992b, p. 56). The new rates included preferential treatment for certain provinces and industrial sectors.

crackdown came in 1985, Hainan officials had spent more than $1 billion on imports of autos and other consumer durables.[47]

Scandals and massive trade deficits caused the government to restrict imports by freezing the foreign exchange retained by government organizations, FTCs, and firms. The central government "borrowed" the foreign exchange to finance central plan imports.[48] MOFTEC reasserted its authority to approve the establishment of new FTCs.[49] In 1986 exports became a top priority to replenish China's depleted foreign exchange reserves and meet debt obligations, and the renminbi cost to the state of earning foreign exchange declined in importance.[50] To promote exports, Beijing devalued the renminbi in January 1985 by eliminating the dual-rate regime and moving the official rate to what had been the internal settlement rate (2.80 yuan to $1); three further devaluations followed in October 1985, July 1986, and November 1986. Local foreign exchange swap markets were also initiated in 1985 (see below), and foreign exchange retention quotas were again increased. The freeze and quota restrictions on the use of retained foreign exchange, however, limited the ability of these actions to reduce the cost of exporting. Therefore the center agreed to resume subsidizing the losses of exporting entities (it is doubtful that it ever had stopped doing so).

Foreign Trade Contracting

In late 1987 and 1988, the center responded to the continuing problems of financial losses in foreign trade and weak export incentives with a new decentralizing reform called "foreign trade contracting." An example of particularistic contracting, the reform

47. Lardy (1992b, p. 60).

48. Lardy (1992b, p. 60). According to a Chinese source quoted by Lardy, during 1980–86 almost one-fifth of the central government's imports were financed by spending the funds retained by exporting firms, FTCs, and local governments. This pattern of the center's taking back with uniform extractions what it had initially given away on a particularistic basis appears in the fiscal relationship between Beijing and the provinces just as it does with foreign exchange retention. The pattern follows the winning political formula of "concentrate benefits, diffuse costs."

49. Xinhua News Agency, April 19, 1985, in JPRS, *China Economic Analysis*, June 5, 1985, p. 119.

50. Zhou, "Foreign Trade Reform Must Be Coordinated with Other Reforms," p. 16.

met the needs of national politicians to win support from the provincial authorities to whom they were largely accountable. Each province (and all national FTCs) negotiated a contract with MOFTEC consisting of three targets: the amount of foreign exchange earnings; the amount of foreign exchange to be remitted to the central government; and a fixed amount of domestic currency the center would provide to subsidize losses on export sales. The contracts signed in 1988 were for three years; in 1991 the provinces were put on a shorter leash when the practice changed to annual renegotiation of contracts. MOFTEC, the Ministry of Finance, and the State Planning Commission formulated the contracted values in bargaining with each province. The State Council had to approve each contract.

From the standpoint of the Ministry of Finance, the trade contracting system represented progress in limiting its financial liability for trade losses. In 1988 it set the aggregate amount of export subsidies at approximately 7 billion yuan, 4 percent of exports. This total was divided among all the provinces and national FTCs signing contracts.[51] This hard budget constraint was intended to force local governments to be responsible for their own profits and losses from trade. The central subsidies for export losses were reportedly eliminated entirely by 1991.

The provinces also welcomed the trade contracting system. Contracting went a long way to free them from central control, especially in combination with the unfreezing and abolition of quota controls on retained hard currency and the drastic shrinking of the central foreign trade plan, which occurred simultaneously. From the provincial perspective, the contract targets were reasonable in that they entailed no loss of benefit from the status quo; like all domestic financial contracts in China, the targets were set according to the previous year's figures. Perhaps most appealing to provincial authorities was the power the new system gave them to assign trade contracts on a particularistic basis to their subordinate FTCs and local governments.[52]

---

51. World Bank (1994, p. 27). According to this source, in 1988 the subsidies required for imports were approximately 20 billion yuan.
52. Lardy (1992b, p. 104).

Although the trade contracting policy achieved both central and provincial support, as a purely administrative mechanism it could not completely compensate for China's price distortions and overvalued currency. Export losses persisted: as of October 1988 the renminbi cost of export earnings stood at 4.15 yuan per U.S. dollar, still substantially higher than the 3.72 official exchange rate at the time.[53] To help offset this disparity, foreign exchange retention rates for provincial and other local governments were increased again, and rates for exports above contract targets were increased to 80 percent.[54] In addition, a system of tax refunds for exporters was introduced.

China's use of administrative decentralization for export promotion, exemplified by the trade contracting system, inhibited the genuine liberalization of the trade regime down to the production-firm level by perpetuating bureaucratic control and strengthening trading companies as monopsonies. Most production firms were required to use FTCs for their exports and were pressured by local governments to use their local FTC rather than one from another province. Some products, such as steel, fertilizer, oil, coal, and tungsten, had to be sold abroad by national FTCs, which collected sizable payoffs from their exclusive rights to exploit the domestic-international price differentials in the products. The government restricted FTCs in their scope: none was permitted to handle all kinds of products or to handle internal trade. Poorly managed FTCs survived because of the absence of competition. Chinese FTCs blocked direct links between buyers and sellers in international trade without necessarily transmitting information about international marketing to the buyers. The fixed, mandatory foreign exchange targets for trading companies, which reflected a continuation of central authority, made them strive to meet these targets without regard to efficiency or profitability. Under these

53. Shan (1989, p. 45).

54. The machinery and electronics industries were favored with special treatment, reflecting the bureaucratic clout of these industries and a central policy of promoting their exports. For machinery, 100 percent of the above-target foreign exchange export revenue could be retained. The electronics and automobile industries could retain 100 percent both under and above the quota. "MOFERT Official on Specific Measures for Reform of the Foreign Trade System," *Economic Reporter* (Hong Kong), April 25, 1988, pp. 11–12, in JPRS, *CAR*, July 12, 1988, p. 27.

conditions, FTCs could not be required to take responsibility for their own profits and losses.[55]

The reformist leadership's strong desire to expand exports and its growing recognition of the shortcomings of administrative decentralization for doing so (and decentralization's bias toward imports) has gradually built support for domestic price liberalization and exchange rate reform. Yet trade decentralization implemented on a particularistic basis has given central and local political authorities an interest in perpetuating an incompletely marketized system.[56]

---

55. World Bank (1994, p. 115).

56. If price distortions are eliminated, a major rationale for particularism—the impossibility of identifying what would be an economically rational pattern of trade or investments—will also disappear.

Chapter 6

Opening the Door Wider

THE economic reforms have been extraordinarily successful at transforming China from a closed economy to a major trading nation. This transformation has been accomplished not by liberalization but by a series of administrative arrangements that achieved a bureaucratic consensus and accommodated the individual incentives of central and local political officials. By keeping their hands on administrative levers, Chinese leaders were able to selectively reward groups that they depend on for political support and that are influential within the selectorate, most notably provincial and heavy industrial officials. Partial opening and halfway marketization represented a political equilibrium.

To open the door further by making foreign exchange freely available and allowing foreign goods to enter the domestic market would present a new political challenge. Liberalization cannot be accomplished by particularistic administrative methods. To the contrary, it involves removing old subsidies and protections and renegotiating the bargain between the central state and various localities and ministries that made halfway reform possible. Without any transformation of communist political institutions, achieving a more universal foreign exchange and trade regime will be much more difficult than carrying out the initial measures.

Yet there are reasons to expect that China will move beyond the political equilibrium of partial reform to liberalize its foreign exchange regime and open its domestic market. Foreign companies and governments are pushing both measures, particularly market

opening; now a major exporter, China fears international retalia-
tion against its products if it fails to comply. Foreign exchange
convertibility and market access are norms of the world trading
system enforced by the International Monetary Fund and GATT.
Beijing's eagerness to join GATT (discussed below) makes international pressure on these issues very effective.

On the domestic front, both central and local officials will be
loath to give up control over access to international business and
foreign exchange. And industrial ministries still rely on protection
from international competition. Yet foreign pressure to liberalize
China's foreign exchange and trading regime will attract some
domestic allies. The particularistic contracting approach to opening has created major financial burdens for the Ministry of Finance and administrative ones for MOFTEC. More significant,
the preferences of key economic groups such as provincial officials
and the machinery and electronics industries have begun to change
over the gradual course of the reforms. They may now be willing to
give up some subsidies and protection to enhance their ability to
compete internationally. Also in favor of increased openness are
the many industrial and bureaucratic groups that hunger for foreign equipment and consumer goods, and for the foreign exchange
needed to buy them.

Reforming the Foreign Exchange Regime

Reflecting the incentives of existing communist political institutions, the Chinese foreign trade reforms initially sought to coun-
teract the export-discouraging effects of an overvalued renminbi,
primarily through administrative allocation of foreign exchange.
Over time, however, some Chinese voices, mostly from Beijing,
began to call for reform of the foreign exchange regime. Because of
high financial losses associated with subsidizing exports under the
foreign exchange retention system, the powerful Ministry of Finance advocated a devaluation of the renminbi and limits on how
much firms could spend in renminbi to generate foreign exchange
from exports. The central foreign trade ministry also favored a
more realistic exchange rate to aid it in achieving a favorable

balance of trade.[1] A new generation of Chinese foreign trade economists and World Bank experts also recognized that even generous foreign exchange retention rates did not provide effective export incentives in the face of the overvalued currency and the profits that could be made selling domestically (derived from the demand produced by high domestic growth rates and high domestic prices for manufactured goods). Despite all the new export incentives, the overvalued currency continued to favor imports over exports. Moreover, almost everyone could recognize the inefficiencies of a system that allowed a company or local government to retain the foreign exchange they earned from exports but prohibited them from selling the foreign exchange to companies or localities wanting to import. Overall, foreign exchange reform did not spark the opposition of key domestic groups the way the market opening issue did, and it even garnered some support.

Although the impetus for reform of the foreign exchange regime came primarily from outside China, the international demands for it were by no means as consistent or insistent as the international demands for market opening. The most forceful demand for convertibility came from foreign investors who wanted to sell on the domestic market and repatriate their profits in hard currency. Under the dual-rate system, joint ventures were penalized because their capital investment was calculated at the higher official rate and their local profits were exchanged for dollars at the lower swap market rate. As for international institutions, although the International Monetary Fund advocated convertibility, it would accept some degree of exchange controls. Joining GATT did not require full convertibility, although dual rates for trading activities, often viewed as export subsidies, were an obstacle to membership. The United States, already running a trade deficit of approximately $20 billion with China, complained out of one side of its mouth

1. A 1984 rule prohibited the inclusion in the export plan of any product with a foreign exchange cost above 5 yuan per dollar of foreign exchange earnings. Lardy (1992b, pp. 100, 119–20). Powerful central government agencies are not always defenders of the status quo and may support reforms that help them achieve organizational goals. For similar reasons, the State Planning Commission favors domestic price reform because low within-plan prices for raw and semifinished products make it difficult for the SPC to carry out its procurement plan for these products; according to Lardy, however, the SPC was skeptical about devaluation.

about dual exchange rates and from the other side warned China about too-rapid devaluation.[2] Chinese central trade officials nevertheless promoted reform of the foreign exchange regime by portraying it as imposed on the country by GATT or "international standards."[3]

Devaluation

In response to international and domestic demands for a reform of the foreign exchange regime, Chinese leaders gradually devalued their currency and created an officially sanctioned swap market for foreign exchange. Devaluation began in 1981 with the adoption of a special internal settlement rate of 2.8 yuan to $1 U.S. for foreign trade transactions. Unlike previous exchange rates, which were pegged to relative prices of a basket of Chinese consumer goods in China (where they are underpriced because of state subsidies) and in international cities, this exchange rate was pegged to the cost of earning foreign exchange in various world markets.[4] According to Nicholas Lardy, although the new internal exchange rate made exports profitable, imports produced unprecedented losses and in a few years exports were generating losses again as well. As a result, losses during 1981–84, when the dual rates existed, were still substantial. The growth in exports, moreover, proved to be disappointing because even with the 2.8 yuan rate the incentives to sell abroad were weak.[5] The creation of dual

2. Carl Goldstein, "Renminbi's Rough Ride," *Far Eastern Economic Review,* August 13, 1992, p. 51.
3. *Wen Wei Po* (Hong Kong), October 27, 1993, p. 2, in Foreign Broadcast Information Service, *Daily Report: China,* October 29, 1993, p. 34. (Hereafter FBIS, *China.*) A People's Bank of China official acknowledged that GATT required only free conversion of the renminbi in trade. Yang Fan, "Director of the Finance Research Institute of the People's Bank of China Says that the Central Government Has Been Ready for Dealing with the Possibility of Exchange Rate Fluctuations," *Wen Wei Po* (Hong Kong), January 3, 1994, in FBIS, *China,* January 5, 1994, p. 31.
4. Lardy (1992b, p. 67). A Chinese source clarifies that this method pegs the renminbi to a basket of other currencies, each weighted by its importance in China's foreign dealings and on the trend of its relative value. Chen Biaoru, "On the Issues of the Pegged Exchange Rate, Flexible Exchange Rate, and the Renminbi Exchange Rate," *Nankai Economic Journal,* no. 6 (December 1990), pp. 3–10, in Joint Publications Research Service, *CAR,* 91-018, p. 62. (Hereafter JPRS.)
5. Lardy (1992b, pp. 71–73).

exchange rates also made China the target of international economic complaints for the first time. In its annual consultations with China's so-called central bank, the People's Bank of China, the International Monetary Fund told the bank that long-term use of dual exchange rates violated IMF standards. Firms in the United States, one of China's largest export markets, filed several complaints claiming that the internal rate was a form of export subsidy.

Responding pragmatically to these problems and pressures, the State Council decided as of January 1, 1985, to eliminate the dual exchange rates and devalue the official rate to the internal settlement rate of 2.8 yuan.[6] Since then, the government has devalued the renminbi five times, often by substantial increments (13 percent in 1986, 21.2 percent in 1989, and 9.57 percent in 1990). As of 1993 the official exchange rate stood at 5.69 yuan to $1 U.S. These exchange rate adjustments had two objectives: to compensate for the effects of inflation on domestic prices and to expand exports and reduce imports in order to resolve the balance of payments deficit and decline in foreign exchange reserves that have existed since 1985.[7]

According to Chinese sources, these devaluations were not effective in enhancing enterprise export incentives. As one analyst frankly stated, "Five rounds of currency devaluation have done nothing to improve terms of trade."[8] Under the contract system, foreign trading companies had to be more concerned with meeting their foreign exchange quotas than earning profits.[9] Any benefits they did receive from devaluation they kept for themselves instead of sharing them with production enterprises. Moreover, in a domestic economy that was growing rapidly with prices rising,

6. The official rate already had been readjusted to 2.3 yuan in 1984.
7. Li Xunlei, "Effects of China's Current Exchange Rate Policies on Foreign Trade," *Finance and Economics Research*, no. 2 (February 1991), pp. 47–49, in JPRS, *CAR*, 91-032, June 13, 1991, p. 55.
8. Li, "Effects of China's Current Exchange Rate Policies on Foreign Trade." The quote may be mistranslated because "terms of trade" are determined by changes in international prices and not by domestic actions like currency devaluation.
9. Wen Jianjun, "Suggestions on Measures to Offset the Adverse Initial Effects of the Reduced Exchange Rate on the Economy," *International Trade Journal*, no. 7 (July 1990), p. 31, in JPRS, *CAR*, 90-081, October 31, 1990, p. 24.

big-step devaluations were mostly catch-up moves that had little marginal effect on exports. Some critics argued that devaluations also fueled the inflation that plagues the Chinese economic system in a cyclical pattern by raising the cost of imports and stimulating exporters' demand for primary products.[10] Lardy disputes this argument and concludes that devaluation had little dampening effect on imports because it was not communicated through domestic prices of imported goods until import prices began to be freed up in the latter half of the 1980s.[11] The failure of exchange rate adjustments to accomplish their purposes in the first half of the decade can be explained by the persistence of administrative controls that prevented the change in currency prices from governing the behavior of economic actors.[12]

Foreign Exchange Markets

The establishment of a parallel foreign exchange market by means of local swap centers, which began with "experiments" in Shenzhen in 1985 and Shanghai in 1986 and was extended throughout the country in 1988, was aimed at improving export incentives by making the use of foreign exchange more efficient and at satisfying the demand of foreign-funded firms for a way to convert their domestic currency earnings to foreign exchange. Under the foreign exchange retention system, foreign exchange remained scarce: central agencies perceived foreign exchange as highly dispersed, hoarded in small quantities by exporting companies and local governments, but from the bottom-up perspective, it looked like the central government continued to concentrate and

10. Chen Zhihong and Luo Shile, "Effect of Reduced Exchange Rate on Export Trade," *International Trade Journal*, no. 7 (July 1990), pp. 29–30, in JPRS, *CAR*, 90-081, October 31, 1990, pp. 22, 23.

11. Lardy (1992b, p. 119).

12. "In China, a new order containing a planned commodity economy has not yet been established, while market mechanisms cannot function properly, disrupted as they are by all sorts of noneconomic factors. Under these circumstances, there is a much greater tendency for an exchange rate policy to backfire than in a market economy. Moreover, in China both foreign trade and financial exchange are under state control. For all practical purposes there is no real foreign exchange market. Basically domestic prices and international prices bear no direct relationship to one another. . . . All this limits the effectiveness of exchange rate as a tool of economic leverage in terms of time, extent, and frequency." Li, "Effects of China's Current Exchange Rate Policies on Foreign Trade."

reallocate the lion's share. Both sides agreed that horizontal movement of foreign exchange would increase the value of retained foreign exchange and improve efficiency of its use. In 1988, when the exchange rate was two-thirds more than the official exchange rate of 3.7, any unit with access to the swap markets would also have had a much stronger incentive to export.[13]

The swap market was also intended to provide information for future adjustments in the official exchange rate. Since 1991 the official rate has been a managed float adjusted frequently on the basis of international and domestic developments, one of the most important of which is the swap market rate.[14] The ultimate goal was merging the swap market and official rates into a marketized official rate by gradually narrowing the spread between the two rates. During 1991 that goal appeared to be in sight as the spread narrowed to less than 0.5 yuan by the end of the year.

Beginning in 1992, however, the swap market rate began to diverge from the stable official rate. In the spring of 1993 the value of the renminbi dropped precipitously on the swap market, falling to a rate of 11 yuan to the dollar in June, almost double the official rate of 5.7.[15] This shock represented a major setback in the effort to marketize the official exchange rate. As one MOFTEC official said with regret, "We seem to have lost a chance when the gap between the official rate and the swap market rate was quite narrow earlier last year."[16] The reasons for the renminbi's sudden drop in value on the swap market highlight the persistent harmful effects of administrative decentralization and particularism on Chinese markets.

13. Zhang Guanghua and Wang Dongmin, "Establishing China's Foreign Exchange Market," *Economic Research*, no. 5 (May 1987), pp. 26, 71, in JPRS, *CAR*, 87-035, August 18, 1987, pp. 74–75; He Xiaosong, "Establish a National Foreign Exchange Market, Promote Strategic Role of Foreign Trade," *International Trade Journal*, no. 6 (1986), pp. 7–12, in JPRS, *China Economic Affairs*, 87-035, August 18, 1987, p. 46; Lardy (1992b, p. 58).

14. Wang Zixian, "An Analysis of Fluctuation Trend of Renminbi Exchange Rate," *Economic Reference News*, July 5, 1993, p. 4, in FBIS, *China*, August 4, 1993, p. 26.

15. The People's Bank of China had imposed a ceiling on swap markets of 8 yuan to the dollar in February 1993, but removed it in early June when the ceiling proved only to drive firms into the black market. Wang, "Analysis of Fluctuation Trend of Renminbi Exchange Rate."

16. Ren Kan, "China Promises to Unify Its Dual Exchange Rates," *China Daily Business Weekly*, June 27, 1993, p. 1, in FBIS, *China*, June 29, 1993, p. 47.

The swap markets, called foreign exchange adjustment centers, were established by the State Administration of Exchange Control, the central governmental agency authorized to manage foreign exchange in China. In 1986 this agency was placed under the People's Bank of China, which, although formally designated as China's central bank, is widely acknowledged to be lacking in professional competence and institutional autonomy. The bank's macroeconomic policies and its management of foreign exchange markets follow the bidding of Communist Party and government leaders.

The bank managed the swap markets in a manner that mirrored its own administrative divisions, which are organized by province. There was no national swap market, merely a collection of provincial and municipal swap markets. In the first wave of foreign exchange adjustment centers, fifty-seven were established: one in each of the twenty-nine provincial level units and one in each of the fourteen open cities, the four SEZs, and the ten cities that are treated as separate entities under the national plan.[17] By 1993 there were over one hundred centers, but they had different local prices and were not properly linked to each other.[18] Local officials discouraged companies and firms from trading outside their home locale and excluded nonlocals from trading in their markets. Local protectionism and blockading created interference and prevented the building of a nationwide foreign exchange market.[19] The geographic balkanization of the foreign exchange market was exacerbated by the lack of an interbank market or a national auction for foreign exchange.

Local administrative interference in the swap markets often took the form of selective access. From their beginnings in 1985–86, the criteria for access to the swap markets were ambiguous and

17. Yowell (1988, p. 10). Even before the formal establishment of the centers, many cities and provinces had been helping enterprises exchange currencies at negotiated rates on an ad hoc basis.

18. Ren, "China Promises to Unify Its Dual Exchange Rates."

19. Gu Limin and Ji Wenxiu, "Tentative Ideas for Improving Foreign Exchange Retention System," *International Trade Journal*, no. 11 (November 1990), pp. 52–53, in JPRS, *CAR*, 91-013, March 6, 1991, p. 65; Wang Ziguang and Zhou Guofang, "Several Problems about the Direction of Renminbi Exchange Rate System Reform," *International Trade Journal*, no. 7 (July 1991), pp. 2–6, in JPRS, *CAR*, 91-060, October 30, 1991, p. 30.

largely locally determined. When the swap market was established in Shanghai, it was limited to foreign investment enterprises. The Shenzhen market, in contrast, allowed all foreign and Chinese enterprises (including those of interior provinces) to participate; unlike other cities, Shenzhen also permitted individuals to buy and sell on the market.[20] Foreign investment enterprises found access to swap markets varying from city to city. As of 1988 most U.S. and foreign manufacturers were continuing to keep their investment projects relatively small (under $5 million) to limit their exposure until their ability to convert renminbi earnings to foreign exchange was more certain.[21]

Not every firm or company was allowed to participate in the foreign exchange adjustment centers (in 1992, 49 percent of China's foreign exchange used for imports was bought in the swap markets).[22] Enterprises had to receive several bureaucratic approvals from local government agencies (regarding the source of the hard currency earnings and their intended use) before entering the swap market. Each of these permissions created potential opportunities for local officials to reward themselves.

As a result of their lack of integration and their particularistic access, many swap markets were dominated by small traders. (Large traders often have import uses for their export earnings and do not need the market.) According to one Chinese official, it was hard to find a swap market transaction of more than $100,000 U.S. Small traders are prone to be influenced by rumors, which helps explain the drastic drop in the value of the renminbi in the first half of 1993. Also influenced by rumors was the trading behavior of individuals, who under Guangdong rules were permitted to trade in the local swap market.[23]

20. Yao Ximin and Zhong Xin, "Foreign Exchange Redistribution Center Set Up to Encourage Foreign Investment," *Guoji Shangbao*, November 13, 1986, p. 1, in JPRS, *China Economic Affairs*, 87-052, March 4, 1987, p. 66; Hu Zhimin, "SEZ Foreign Exchange Markets Gradually Taking Shape; City's Regulated Prices for Foreign Exchange Completely Deregulated," *Shenzhen Special Zone Journal*, November 22, 1986, p. 1, in JPRS, *China Economic Affairs*, 87-016, p. 41.

21. Yowell (1988, p. 11); Frisbie (1988, p. 24).

22. "Foreign Exchange Market Regulations Made Public," Xinhua News Agency, April 15, 1993, in FBIS, *China*, April 16, 1963, p. 41.

23. Kent Chen, "Guangzhou Takes Steps to Effectively Float Yuan," *South China Morning Post* (Hong Kong), April 13, 1993, p. 1, in FBIS, *China*, April 13, 1993, p. 18.

These rumors, which provoked individuals, small traders, and even some large traders to hoard their foreign exchange and to drive up its value on the swap market, predicted an imminent move by China to join GATT and to make its currency fully convertible. The rumors had a basis in the expectations of the national government itself. During 1992–93 the PRC intensified its efforts to join GATT and signed a market access agreement with the United States that it believed would accelerate its entry to GATT. People anticipated that when China joined GATT, there would be a huge increase in available imports. Especially under conditions of domestic price inflation, it was rational to hold hard currency for purchasing these foreign goods.[24] And a decision to make the currency convertible as part of China's entry into GATT would drastically devalue the renminbi, also creating a boon for those who held hard currency. In February 1993 the director of the State Administration of Exchange Control stated publicly that the goal was to make the renminbi a convertible currency, beginning first on the current items and then on capital items.[25]

Also contributing to the downward pressure on the renminbi in swap markets was the national policy announced in early 1993 permitting individuals to take out 6,000 yuan in renminbi to Hong Kong.[26] An informal market trading Hong Kong dollars for renminbi was formed in Hong Kong; it was governed by local supply and was rife with speculation. (According to one Beijing official, the renminbi was trading at 12 yuan to the dollar in Hong Kong in 1993.) The change in PRC swap market rates appeared to follow the much smaller Hong Kong market, reflecting the extensive monetary integration between Hong Kong and the mainland.

24. Wang, "Analysis of Fluctuation Trend of Renminbi Exchange Rate," pp. 26–27. The surge in imports and price inflation that accompanied economic overheating in late 1992 and 1993 also contributed to the decline of the renminbi on the swap market.

25. Wang Yinghui, "Yin Jieyan Says the Foreign Exchange Control Structure Reform Goal Is to Turn Renminbi into a Convertible Currency," *Economics Reference News*, February 16, 1993, p. 1, in FBIS, *China*, March 5, 1993, p. 30. There was some suspicion in Hong Kong and abroad that the government had caused the depreciation of the renminbi on the swap market to accelerate the currency's devaluation before China's entry to GATT.

26. Chen, "Guangzhou Takes Steps"; Henny Sender, "Convert Your Renminbi," *Far Eastern Economic Review*, April 1, 1993, p. 67.

The swap market value of thè renminbi rose during the second half of 1993 to 8.7 yuan to the dollar, thanks partially to new State Council rules that prohibited firms from hoarding foreign exchange quotas.[27] A sizable gap remained between swap market and official rates, however, so that combining the rates would involve a substantial devaluation.

A Major Transformation

By the fall of 1993 it appeared likely that China would soon transform its foreign exchange regime by merging the swap market and official rates and moving toward renminbi convertibility. Chinese domestic demands for such a transformation had increased over time. The international demands from the IMF, the United States, and foreign investors were reinforced by MOFTEC, the Ministry of Finance, and the expanding group of provinces, FTCs, and enterprises engaged in exporting. Even the State Administration of Exchange Control and the People's Bank of China, which previously had favored the maintenance of foreign exchange controls and a very gradual move toward convertibility, appeared to have changed their minds by fall 1993.[28] Chen Yuan, a powerful vice governor of the bank, stated in October 1993 that the renminbi could begin to float as early as 1994.[29] Although local officials, who benefit from control of access to scarce foreign exchange in swap markets, stood to lose potential benefits by making foreign exchange universally available and more plentiful, they still retained many other economic controls; there was no

27. Firms were required to use quotas they received in the first half of 1993 before the end of September, and any quotas obtained in the second half of 1993 had to be used within six months. If not used, the quotas would be purchased back by the state at the weighted average price in the market. Ren Kan, "Renminbi Gains Lost Ground on Swap Marts," *China Daily Business Weekly,* July 4, 1993, p. 1, in FBIS, *China,* July 7, 1993, pp. 34–35.

28. In April 1993 SAEC Director Yin Jieyan emphasized the point that rejoining GATT does not require scrapping controls on exchanges and exchange rates. Yin Jieyan, "On Exchange Rate Policy and Issues Concerning Exchange Control," *People's Daily,* April 8, 1993, in FBIS, *China,* April 30, 1993, p. 20.

29. Agence France-Press (Hong Kong), October 18, 1993, in FBIS, *China,* October 18, 1993, p. 42. In May 1993 MOFTEC officials had promised the GATT working party on China that it would introduce a single exchange rate system within five years. Ren, "China Promises to Unify Its Dual Exchange Rates."

evidence that they vehemently opposed reform of the foreign exchange regime.

In December 1993 the government announced its intention to unify the exchange rates, standardize the nationwide foreign exchange quotation mechanism with the Shanghai rate as the standard, cancel the foreign exchange retention system, and eliminate the foreign exchange certificates (the parallel currency used by foreigners traded at official exchange rates) to allow nonresidents to trade foreign exchange at market rates. Although the exchange rates were unified at the lower swap market rate of 8.7 yuan to the dollar on January 1, 1994, the full transformation to a floating-rate market was postponed until April 1 because of the complexities of unifying swap markets into a national bank–based foreign exchange market and creating an interbank market.[30] Originally the intention was to eliminate all the swap centers accessed by official approvals. By March, however, People's Bank of China officials announced that the swap centers would remain open for foreign-funded ventures to buy and sell their foreign exchange there instead of at the banks.[31] The foreign-funded companies, fearful of exchange rate risk under an untested Chinese system, lobbied hard through MOFTEC for this exception to the new arrangements. Convertibility is limited to trading activities, as required by GATT. The conversion of currency from nontrade current account activities is expected to take about six years.[32] Capital account convertibility is not anticipated because "there is a great domestic demand for capital and the outflow of domestic capital through free conversion is not allowed."[33]

Administrative control of access to exchange markets is not entirely eliminated by the 1994 reform. An exporting enterprise needs "a valid certificate to convert renminbi for foreign exchange provided its operation meets the requirements of the state indus-

30. "Foreign Exchange Rate Unification Planned," Kyodo News Agency (Tokyo), December 25, 1993, in FBIS, *China,* December 27, 1993, p. 54.

31. Kennis Chu, "Foreign Exchange Swap Centers to Close by April," *South China Sunday Morning Post,* January 30, 1994, p. 1, in FBIS, *China,* February 1, 1994, p. 38; Ren Kan, "Bank Trade to Centralize Most Foreign Exchange," *China Daily,* March 29, 1994, p. 1, in FBIS, *China,* March 29, 1994, p. 36.

32. "Renminbi Expected Convertible in Six Years," *China Daily,* March 7, 1994, p. 2.

33. Yang, "Director of the Finance Research Institute."

trial policy." Presumably this certificate consists of the "import quota, license, or other import authorization issued by the departments concerned" described in the new regulations.[34]

Chinese reform economists express disappointment at the limitations of the 1994 foreign exchange market reform. Access to exchange markets remains under the administrative control of officials. The perpetuation of the swap markets for foreign-funded enterprises reinforces a lack of international confidence in the Chinese banking system and foreign exchange market. The market exchange rate of 8.7 yuan to the dollar has remained stable only because, contrary to official statements, the bank intervenes actively in both the exchange market and the swap markets.[35]

Despite its limitations, the reform of foreign exchange management moves in the direction of liberalizing the Chinese trading system and creating a level playing field among regions, industries, and firms. It was accomplished with greater ease than is likely with the next challenge, opening the domestic market.

Opening the Domestic Market

Compared with foreign exchange reforms, opening the domestic market involves more intense international pressure and more controversial domestic implications. Although China has run a global trade deficit in seven of the past ten years, it has large surpluses with the United States and the European Community, its two most influential and assertive trading partners. To avert retaliatory action from the United States under section 301 of the 1988 Trade Act, China signed an agreement with the United States in October 1992 to lower tariffs and remove import barriers such as quotas, import restrictions, import licensing requirements,

34. "Wu Yi Discusses Foreign Trade, Exchange Reform," Xinhua News Agency, December 30, 1993, in FBIS, *China,* January 4, 1994, p. 30; "Central Bank's New Reforms of Foreign Exchange System," *China Daily,* January 16, 1994, p. 4, in FBIS, *China,* January 18, 1994, p. 22

35. "Official 'Optimistic' about Stability of Yuan," *Zhongguo Xinwen She,* May 9, 1994, in FBIS, *China,* May 10, 1994, p. 27. Also see Shuang Mu, "Stable Renminbi Expected through Rest of the Year," *China Daily,* June 13, 1994, p.1.

and import controls. Entry to GATT requires the abolition of these import barriers and the lowering of tariffs.[36]

Removing Trade Restrictions

Although China has been progressively reducing its tariffs to meet these international requirements, removing administrative controls on imports will be politically difficult. Since 1979 Chinese policies have been explicitly aimed at promoting exports while protecting domestic industries. No one in China has made a secret of its continued protectionism.[37] As an "infant exporter," China has both offered special inducements to exporters and protected domestic industries from international competition, a strategy previously adopted by Korea and Taiwan that has been labeled "protected export promotion."[38] As of 1988 import licenses were required for fifty-three products that together accounted for 45 percent of China's total imports.[39] In March 1994 a trade official estimated the number of import items subject to quotas or requiring licenses at about fifty, most of them capital goods, including eighteen electronic and machinery products. The official announced that the country pledged to cut the number of products needing import licenses by at least two-thirds and to reduce tariffs by 40 percent to meet the

36. During 1993 the PRC twice reduced the import tariffs on 2,800 categories of commodities, including raw materials and machinery. It also announced a list of tariff reductions for agricultural products and service trades. It has declared its intention to meet the required tariff level of 30 percent for nonagricultural products before reentering GATT. He Chang, "Article Views Prospects of Admission to GATT 'This Year,' " *Zhongguo Tongxun She* (Hong Kong), March 7, 1994, in FBIS, *China*, March 17, 1994, p. 2.

37. Liu Mohai, "The Question of Renminbi Exchange Rate," *Economic Research*, no. 11 (November 1988), pp. 53, 59, in JPRS, *CAR*, 89-013, February 9, 1989, p. 46; Zhang Yansheng, "Study of Relationship between Trade Strategy and Economic Development," *Economic Research*, no. 11 (November 20, 1990), pp. 69–75, in JPRS, *CAR*, 91-017, March 26, 1991, p. 68.

38. Koves and Marer (1991, p. 24).

39. Yang Yuntian, "China's Import and Export Licensing System," *International Trade Journal*, no. 5 (May 1990), pp. 2–4, in JPRS, *CAR*, 90-071, September 21, 1990, p. 73. The products included 23 capital goods and raw materials including steel products, lumber, rubber, petroleum, and wool; 24 machinery and electronics including automobiles, televisions, camcorders, and processing equipment; and 6 other. A U.S. expert states that these 53 products are actually 572 categories of goods, and that in addition 234 categories of goods are subject to bans and 52 to quotas. Massey (1992, p. 10).

requirements for GATT entry and to phase out all quota restrictions by 1997.[40]

One of the most difficult forms of administrative protection to
eliminate will be the special treatment of the powerful machinery
and electronics industries. Unlike other industries, for which import controls fall under MOFTEC's jurisdiction, since the advent
of the open policy these industries have had the special privilege of
managing directly all imports of machinery and electronics equipment. Every company or enterprise that wants to import equipment must obtain permission not just from its local trade and
finance departments but also from the special State Office for
Import and Export of Machinery and Electronic Products. This
office was authorized under import-substitution policies to deny
approval for imported equipment manufactured by a domestic
producer. It also enforced safety and quality standards for imports
and administered machinery and electronics import quotas.[41]

Under the market access agreement with the United States,
China has promised to eliminate import-substitution trade restrictions like the one applied to machinery and electronics, which also
would be unacceptable under GATT. At a May 1993 work conference, machinery and electronics officials were told they had to
restrict the scope of control over machinery and electrical product
imports and eliminate by two-thirds the number of products subject to examination and approval. The conference engaged in
"intense efforts" to draft a document on how machinery and
electronics products would be imported in the future.[42] What they
came up with allowed the continuation of the State Office for
Import and Export of Machinery and Electronic Products and
many of its powers except scrutiny of imports on the grounds of
import substitution. The import-substitution dimension in the
future would be handled in the following fashion: "Machinery and
electronic products whose production technologies have been do-

40. Wang Yong, "China Sets a Date to End Quotas on Imports," *China Daily*, March
30, 1994, p. 1.

41. Jiang Jun and Zhang Xi, "Machinery Import Rules to Be Eased for GATT,"
Xinhua News Agency, May 16, 1993, in FBIS, *China*, May 25, 1993, pp. 28–29; "Interim
Procedures Governing the Import of Machinery and Electronic Products," Xinhua News
Agency, October 10, 1993, in FBIS, *China*, October 25, 1993, pp. 42–45.

42. Jiang and Zhang, "Machinery Import Rules to Be Eased for GATT."

mestically developed or imported but whose industrial application is still in an initial stage and whose development needs to be accelerated by the state, shall be listed in a special products catalogue for importation mainly through open bidding. SOIEMEA will issue import certificates in accordance with the results of the bidding."[43] A small number of machinery and electronic products "which, if imports are excessive, can seriously jeopardize the development of the relevant industries in the PRC or can directly affect the adjustment of the industrial structure and product mix" will be subject to import quota control according to prevailing international practice.[44]

Many industrial ministry officials are extremely worried about having to face competition from foreign producers. They view China's entry to GATT as a "disaster [that] will soon befall them."[45] Domestic textile manufacturers are thrilled by the prospect of joining GATT and expanding their export markets. The textile industry has little clout in national policymaking, however. The much more influential machinery and electronics industries fear competition with imported home appliances and automobiles.[46]

Objectives for Rejoining GATT

In the face of such powerful skeptics, why did China's leaders commit the country to rejoining GATT? China made application in 1986: its movement toward membership was set back by inter-

43. "Interim Procedures Governing the Import of Machinery and Electronic Products," p. 43. According to another source, there are 171 products in this category. Chen Yun, "New System Governs Machinery, Electronic Imports," Xinhua News Agency, January 18, 1994, in FBIS, *China,* January 28, 1994, p. 39.

44. "Machinery, Electronic Import Rules Promulgated," *Zhongguo Tongxun She* (Hong Kong), November 11, 1993, in FBIS, *China,* November 12, 1993, p. 57. According to another source, there are 18 products in this category, including automobiles, motorcycles, video cameras, computers, and air conditioners. Chen, "New System Governs Machinery, Electronic Imports."

45. Pi Zi, "Imported Goods Are Not a Scourge," *People's Daily,* January 17, 1993, p. 2, in FBIS, *China,* February 4, 1993, p. 28.

46. Liu Li, "Impact of China's Admission to GATT on Its Yarn and Cloth Exports," *Guoji Shangbao,* January 30, 1993, p. 3, in FBIS, *China,* February 22, 1993, pp. 32–34; Pi Shuyi, "Three Questions on Rejoining the GATT," *People's Daily,* February 16, 1993, p. 2, in FBIS, *China,* February 24, 1993, pp. 30–31; Geng Zhaojie, "Where Is the Road Leading to China's Readmission to GATT?" *Guoji Shangbao,* March 27, 1993, p. 3, in FBIS, *China,* April 14, 1993, pp. 27–29.

national condemnation of the Tiananmen crackdown in 1989, and since 1992 it has reintensified its efforts to join. As a major trading nation, China certainly would benefit from the wider access to export markets and the availability of international arbitration that accompany GATT membership. And reform-minded Chinese officials saw the issue of GATT entry as a lever to promote domestic market reforms. When Chinese officials discuss GATT membership and try to persuade people of its value, however, it is obvious that their desire to rejoin the organization is motivated primarily by political-diplomatic objectives, not economic ones. This has been particularly true since 1989.

The PRC government wants to gain admission to GATT ahead of Taiwan, which applied to join in 1990. Beijing insists that it enter first, claiming that the PRC, not Taiwan, is the legitimate heir to China's original seat on GATT, which it received as one of the founders of the organization in 1947. There are a number of knotty international legal issues surrounding this question of Chinese representation in GATT.[47] It has become a matter of national pride that Beijing rejoins the organization before Taipei, although it will not oppose membership for Taipei.[48] The race between the mainland and Taiwan to join GATT has intensified since the signing of the Uruguay round document in December 1993; when the new World Trade Organization replaces GATT in January 1995, all the GATT signatories will automatically become founding members. Both areas care intensely about obtaining that special status.[49]

An equally important element in China's drive to join GATT was its leaders' desire to rid themselves of the annual review of their most favored nation (MFN) trade status by the U.S. government. Every year since 1989 the U.S. Congress had bashed China's poor human rights record, as well as its weapons sales and trade surplus with the United States. MFN status for China was

47. Cai (1992).

48. The United States is unlikely to treat China's participation in GATT as a reentry, but will probably try to fudge the issue so as not to alienate either the PRC or Taiwan.

49. "China's Restoration of GATT's Seat at Delicate Stage," Xinhua News Agency, December 18, 1993, in FBIS, *China*, December 20, 1993, p. 2; He, "Article Views Prospects of Admssion to GATT 'This Year,'"; Sofia Wu, "Taipei Seeks GATT Membership before 1995," *China News Analysis* (Taipei), December 21, 1993, in FBIS, *China*, December 21, 1993, p. 66.

never retracted, because Congress lacked the votes to override the presidential veto; in 1993 Congress delegated the enforcement of conditions for renewal to the president. Yet having to run the gauntlet every year took a terrible toll on China's self-respect and China-United States relations.

Chinese officials (as well as many Americans) believed that GATT membership guaranteed MFN treatment from all other GATT signatories and that the United States would have to comply.[50] In fact, under GATT rules, article 35 allows any contracting party to opt out of applying GATT tariff schedules to new members and thereby to continue applying discriminatory treatment. In the past, the United States has invoked article 35 to deny MFN status to other communist nations, specifically Romania in 1971 and Hungary in 1973.[51] China is listed by name in the Jackson-Vanik legislation creating the MFN review process; unless Congress cancels or revises the law, it will take precedence over the GATT agreement.[52] If China were to obtain GATT membership, thus demonstrating its commitment to a market economy, members of Congress would certainly view China more favorably, but by no means does this guarantee that they would grant China MFN status permanently and unconditionally. Even though President Clinton renewed China's MFN status and recommended delinking the country's trade status from its human rights policy, this issue can ultimately be decided only by Congress.

During the period of tense Sino-American relations (1989–94), Beijing came to view the issue of GATT membership as a contest with the United States. As PRC leaders see it, the United States keeps moving the goalposts by adding new conditions for GATT

50. Su Jingxiang, "Background and Prospects for China's Application to Reenter GATT," *People's Daily* (overseas edition), June 24, 1993, p. 6, in FBIS, *China*, June 29, 1993, p. 10; Ji Chongwei, "Mutually Complementary, Mutually Beneficial, Seeking Common Interests While Reserving Differences," *Economic Daily*, January 16, 1993, p. 4, in FBIS, *China*, February 2, 1993, p. 4.

51. Mac Cormac (1993, p. 35).

52. Article 35 applies only if the contracting and new parties have not entered into tariff negotiations with each other. The U.S. government, perhaps with this condition in mind, avoided formal tariff negotiations during the negotiations of the October 1992 market access agreement. Article 35 also would permit the United States to deny MFN status to China only if China joins GATT as a new member, not by resuming China's seat. Mac Cormac (1993, p. 35).

entry. In addition to the conditions originally laid down in 1989, the United States set some new ones in 1993, demanding that the renminbi correspond with free exchange rate standards, prohibiting the use of fluctuating exchange rates as a means of trade protection, demanding the abolition of preferential policies for particular localities (presumably including the special economic zones), and demanding uniform tax treatment and the opening of the services market.[53]

The decision to pursue GATT membership was made in a relatively centralized fashion so that it could not be blocked by opposition from industry. According to a senior trade official, GATT decisions were defined as foreign policy issues: the Foreign Ministry, MOFTEC, the Bank of China, the tourist administration, and the SEZ office met and made recommendations directly to senior CCP leaders, thereby bypassing the industrial ministries.

Will China's leadership, having decided for largely political and diplomatic reasons to join GATT, actually enforce policies that open China's domestic market and end the protection for powerful industries such as machinery and electronics? One advantage of maintaining communist institutions during the economic transition is that party and government leaders retain the authority to impose policies from the top down. Under delegation by consensus, when a policy is of great importance to the leaders, they can order the bureaucracy to implement it. If industrial ministers resist, party leaders can simply replace them.

But because party leaders are accountable to the ministers and other officials in the selectorate, they generally prefer not to impose unpopular policies on them. For this reason, Chinese officials, including the leader of the Chinese negotiating team, have suggested that when China joins GATT, it will still be able to protect key (politically powerful) industries.[54] China expects to be able to retain administrative protection of certain industries because it is rejoining GATT (not joining as a new member) and because it is claiming the status of a developing country. At a gathering for factory managers, an official announced that the

53. He, "Article Views Prospects of Admission to GATT 'This Year.'"
54. "Official on Understanding GATT Status Renewal," *Zhongguo Tongxun She* (Hong Kong), February 20, 1993, in FBIS, *China*, March 2, 1993, p. 28.

government had already decided to designate the automobile, chemical, and electronics industries as the main protected industries after the country becomes a GATT member.[55]

The machinery and electronics industries, moreover, may no longer be such staunch opponents of market opening. Their own preferences have been altered by the reform experience since 1979. Imports of assembly lines have enabled them to expand production of profitable consumer appliances and electronic equipment. Most important, they have become exporters with an interest in opening up international markets for their products. In 1992, the machinery and electronics industries contributed 23 percent of China's exports; during 1993 these exports grew by 16.1 percent to hit a record high of $22.71 billion, constituting 24.7 percent of total exports.[56] In 1991, 24 percent of China's television production was exported. In 1993 China exported more cassette tape recorders and black-and-white television sets than any other country in the world.[57] Nowadays, what these industries demand more than protection is an import-export bank to provide government financing for their exports.[58] Chinese exporters of machinery and electronics are concentrated in regions that are at the vanguard of China's new outward orientation and are the least protectionist; Guangdong Province accounted for 60 percent of the country's total exports in these industries in 1993. Seventy-three percent of Chinese machinery and electronics exports flow to the United States,

55. Li Piaomin, "On the Protection of National Infant Industries under GATT," *Guoji Shangbao,* February 20, 1993, p. 3, in FBIS, *China,* March 10, 1993, pp. 37–38; "Automobiles, Chemicals, and Electronic Industries Designated as Protected Industries after China Reenters GATT," *Ming Pao* (Hong Kong), January 29, 1993, p. 9, in FBIS, *China,* February 9, 1993, p. 31.

56. Zhu Ling, "State Plans Bank to Help Foreign Trade," *China Daily Business Weekly,* June 20, 1993, p. 1, in FBIS, *China,* June 21, 1993, p. 55; "Customs Publishes Machinery, Electronic Export Figures," Xinhua News Agency, January 31, 1994, in FBIS, *China,* February 2, 1994, p. 35.

57. Wang Zhaodong and Li Zhengping, "China Should Become a Major Trade Power, Comrade Li Lanqing on Opening Up to the Outside World," *Economics Daily,* January 6, 1993, p. 1, in FBIS, *China,* February 4, 1993, p. 23; Pei Jianfeng, "Appetite Grows for Electronics," *China Daily Business Weekly,* February 14, 1994, p. 3.

58. Zhu, "State Plans Bank to Help Foreign Trade," p. 54; "Tong Zhiguang on Purpose of Export-Import Bank," Beijing Central Television, April 28, 1994, in FBIS, *China,* May 18, 1994, p. 46.

Western Europe, Hong Kong, and Japan; the first two could retaliate if China refuses to lower its import barriers.[59]

This new outward orientation of the powerful machinery and electronics industries, itself a consequence of the post-1979 open policy, is weakening their ministries' resistance to opening the market. Another significant domestic force behind market opening is the multitude of joint venture and local companies hungering for foreign equipment. In 1993 China imported almost $50 billion worth of machinery and electronic products, up 41.7 percent from the previous year and constituting 47.6 percent of total imports.[60] Because of these changes in domestic preferences, strong international pressure from the United States and Europe and China's own desire to quickly join GATT may result in opening China's massive market to foreign products.

59. "Customs Publishes Machinery, Electronic Export Figures."
60. "New System Governs Machinery, Electronic Imports," Xinhua News Agency, January 18, 1994, in FBIS, *China*, January 28, 1994, p. 39.

Chapter 7

The Political Challenge of Deeper Integration

*T*HE distinctive behavior of Chinese communist institutions left its mark on the way China began to open its door to world business after 1979. Foreign investment was drawn in by offering geographic regions preferential treatment to attract investors; this regional particularism produced a bandwagon of support for the open door. Exports were spurred by giving local officials a share of foreign exchange earnings. Even when the first foreign exchange markets were established, local officials were able to authorize access to them selectively.

From an economic perspective, the policies adopted may not have been optimal—resources were wasted in payoffs to local officials and were not allocated efficiently—but they succeeded in building political support for what was, after all, a fundamental turnaround in China's stance toward the world. Groups that began as vociferous opponents of the open policy, such as inland provinces or machinery and electronics industries, started to demand access to its benefits. After a dozen years of gradual reform, bureaucratic preferences were reoriented outward to such an extent that leaders felt they could move the country into GATT and accede to international pressure for exchange rate convertibility and market opening without alienating the groups to whom they were politically accountable.

Having achieved a successful shallow integration with the world economy, China is now becoming the target of international efforts to promote harmonization of standards for internal production processes. As a country that is quite late to develop, China is not allowed any breathing room before the issues of deeper integration such as intellectual property rights, environmental protection, and labor treatment confront it.

Addressing these issues in a manner that satisfies foreign governments, nongovernmental organizations (NGOs), and firms will be extremely difficult for China because it involves strict enforcement of uniform rules affecting domestic economic actors. Previous opening policies obtained political support by providing particularistic treatment to key sectors and regions (especially regions); central leaders tacitly agreed to look the other way while local officials exploited the possibilities this preferential treatment extended to them. Meeting international standards for intellectual property rights, environmental protection, and labor treatment, however, requires central leaders to monitor and regulate the actions of local and ministry officials and firm managers after fifteen years of enlarging their autonomy. Transparency is the antithesis of particularism. Although the center still has the authority to discipline officials by transferring or firing them, central leaders are motivated by their own political ambitions not to alienate local officials. Enforcing standards on the growing number of private, collective, and joint venture firms, which now produce approximately one-half the total industrial output, is both easier and harder than enforcing standards on government bureaucracies and state firms. It is easier because the nonstate firms are not part of the Communist Party selectorate and lack any institutional political voice, and harder because the government has less leverage through supply, finance, or personnel over the nonstate firms.

Enforcement of new international standards for intellectual property, environmental protection, or labor treatment would require central leaders to impose financial and political costs on politically powerful local and industrial officials. The total sum of these costs, particularly for environmental cleanup, would be massive. Moreover, there are no politically influential domestic groups pressing for higher standards. The writers, musicians, and scientists who may identify with the cause of intellectual property rights are members of the intelligentsia, which has been politically marginalized under communism. Although there are rumors of isolated local protests from farmers and fisherman about industrial pollution, the Communist Party prohibits the creation of the type of environmental organizations that have led efforts to clean up the environment in most other countries. In addition, Beijing has severely restricted the access to China of international environmental NGOs. Similarly, although there are reports of widespread labor protests about poor working conditions, independent labor organizations are expressly forbidden and even the official labor union has no permanent voice in the government.

With the strongest domestic political forces lined up on the side of the status quo, the demand for reforms in all three areas comes almost entirely from outside China. As previous experiences in Japan and elsewhere have shown, foreign pressure is usually ineffective without domestic political allies and domestic political institutions that empower these allies. And, as the failure of U.S. efforts to improve China's human rights performance has shown, unilateral foreign efforts to impose new standards on issues that could be construed as matters of cultural taste evoke a nasty xenophobic backlash from Chinese leaders. These leaders use such issues to compete with one another to demonstrate their firm nationalist backbone to their bureaucratic constituencies.

Even if the center might muster the political will to carry out new standards, deteriorating administrative capacity is likely to interfere with enforcement. Before the reform era, Beijing depended on local economic bureaucracies to provide information about how firms were carrying out central policies and on local tax offices to collect national taxes. Since the advent of decentralizing reforms, local officials are less reliable agents because they put local economic interests first. Growing localism has impeded the ability of the center to monitor local activities. To collect national taxes under the new 1994 tax reform, Beijing has been forced to create a Chinese equivalent of the Internal Revenue Service, independent of local influence, which will take years to become fully operative. The national banking system faces a similar challenge to overcome localism.

Intellectual Property Rights

In the case of intellectual property rights, it took the arm-twisting of a Super 301 investigation by the United States to gain Chinese agreement to conform to international standards in 1992. According to the 1992 U.S.-PRC memorandum of understanding, the Chinese government agreed to join the Berne Convention for the Protection of Literary and Artistic Works and the Geneva Phonograms Convention. Under the agreement, computer programs will be protected under the category of literary works. China also agreed to amend its patent law to permit patenting of new pharmaceutical and chemical inventions. One of the problems with this agreement is that China's copyright law (1990) is inconsistent with key rules of the Berne Convention. For example, the copyright law fails to provide exclusive rights over public performances of films and sound recordings. In the memorandum, the Chinese agreed only that when there is a contradiction between the Berne Convention and Chinese law, the Berne Convention will prevail. Many concerned foreigners are skeptical about whether it will be possible to assert rights in China based solely on international treaties.[1]

Another difficult issue for China is the unauthorized use of registered trademarks. Despite a 1982 trademark law and repeated well-publicized fining of firms that have counterfeited overseas trademarks, bogus brand-name merchandise, from M & M candy to Levi jeans, is omnipresent in Chinese cities such as Shanghai.[2] The trademark law was revised in 1993 to give it more teeth.

The Chinese have won praise from Arpad Bogsch, the director general of the World Intellectual Property Organization: "It's remarkable that China has made such rapid progress in a short time. . . . Regarding China's patent system, people from both home and abroad can be confident."[3] The existence of well-established

1. Simone (1992, pp. 9–10).
2. Yu Jianyang, "Protect Intellectual Property Rights and Improve the Investment Environment," *Beijing Review*, June 3, 1991, pp. 31–33; Yu Jianyang, "Steps to Protect Intellectual Property," *Beijing Review*, March 9, 1992, p. 10.
3. Chen Jinwu and Lang Guohua, "China Attaches Great Importance to Protecting Intellectual Property Rights," *Beijing Review*, February 17, 1992, p. 31.

multilateral institutions that enforce international intellectual property rights helped diffuse any backlash against unilateral U.S. pressures, while at the same time the U.S. threat of trade sanctions under the Super 301 complaint focused the attention of the Chinese leaders. At the policy level, the Chinese have been as compliant on the intellectual property rights issue as anyone could expect. They have issued a government white paper on the subject.[4] They have even established intellectual property rights courts in Beijing, Shanghai, Guangzhou, Shenzhen, Xiamen, and Haikou to hear cases on violations of trademarks, copyrights, and patents.[5] These legal institutions provide opportunities for foreign firms to police and penalize violations of their proprietary rights in the absence of an effective domestic enforcement effort.

The actual enforcement of the new rules on intellectual property rights has been extremely unsatisfactory, however, from the standpoint of foreign companies and the U.S. government. The United States was estimated to have lost $827 million in 1993 to Chinese piracy of its movies, music, software, and books.[6] The U.S. trade representative threatened to impose trade sanctions against continued Chinese piracy, and on June 30, 1994, gave Beijing only six more months to solve the piracy problem.[7] Chinese foreign trade minister Wu Yi admitted to uneven enforcement of intellectual property rights and attributed the problem to the country's "vast territory and large population."[8] In spring and summer 1994, Beijing ordered city and provincial governments to carry out a series of well-publicized raids against compact disc and laser disc pirates in Beijing, Jiangsu, and Guangdong, the most conspicuous offenders among the provinces.[9] Continuous local enforcement of

4. "White Paper on Property Protection," *China Daily*, June 17, 1994, p. 1.

5. Ma Chenguang, "More Courts to Protect Trademarks and Patents," *China Daily*, March 29, 1994, p. 1.

6. Carl Goldstein, "Pirates' Lair," *Far Eastern Economic Review*, May 19, 1994, p. 55.

7. Thomas L. Friedman, "China Faces U.S. Sanctions in Electronic Copyright Piracy," *New York Times*, July 1, 1994, p. C2.

8. "Property Rights Protection Stressed," Xinhua News Agency, January 28, 1994, in Foreign Broadcast Information Service, *Daily Report: China*, January 28, 1994, p. 30. (Hereafter FBIS, *China*.)

9. "Shenzhen Officials Raid Vendors Selling Pirated CDs," *Zhongguo Tongxun She* (Hong Kong), April 19, 1994, in FBIS, *China*, April 21, 1994, p. 49; "Guangdong Sweep against Pirated Compact, Laser Discs," *Wen Wei Po* (Hong Kong), April 20, 1994, in FBIS, *China*, April 21, 1994, p. 47; "Assault on Disc Pirates Picks Up Momentum," *China Daily*, June 13, 1994.

antipiracy laws remains elusive, however.[10] Another obstacle to effective implementation is the refusal of various industrial ministries and departments to abandon the lucrative pirating business despite a new regulation requiring that all disc duplication business be put under the jurisdiction of departments directly related to the industry.[11] Observers have noted a great deal of bureaucratic conflict over the issue among various ministries.[12] Central authorities find it difficult to muster the political will and administrative capacity to crack down on local and ministry officials upon whom they are politically dependent.

Environmental Protection

China will have an even harder time tackling its environmental problems. More than forty years of giving policy priority to rapid industrial growth has created severe air and water pollution and soil erosion. Coal provides 76 percent of China's energy, and most Chinese coal is high in sulfur and low in quality. Industrial air pollution generates acid rain that falls on China and its East Asian neighbors. The huge scale of the country's coal-burning industrial economy makes China a major contributor to global environmental problems as well. China's production of chlorofluorocarbons placed it ninth in the world in 1991.[13] According to its 1990 figures, China ranked fourth after the United States, USSR, and Brazil in contributions to greenhouse gases, mainly because of burning coal.[14] Because of the massive scale and high growth rate

10. According to a Hong Kong source, "The main reason pirated CDs are in vogue in the mainland is that some unscrupulous businessmen from Hong Kong and Taiwan, taking advantage of the weak sense of copyright and loose law enforcement in some localities in the mainland, have bribed concerned local officials or solicited business for persons in charge of CD manufacturing plants so as to seek the latter's tacit approval in producing pirated CDs in an almost open way." "Daily Describes Upsurge of Pirated CDs," *Wen Wei Po* (Hong Kong), April 20, 1994, in FBIS, *China*, April 21, 1994, p. 23.

11. "Authorities Issue Circular on Audio, Video Piracy," Xinhua News Agency, April 19, 1994, in FBIS, *China*, April 21, 1994, pp. 22–23.

12. Simone (1992, p. 11).

13. Sandy Hendry, "Policy Reform When It Suits," *Far Eastern Economic Review*, October 29, 1992, p. 43.

14. Robert Nadelson, "The Ruined Earth," *Far Eastern Economic Review*, September 19, 1991, p. 39.

of its industrial economy, many foreign environmentalists consider China to be the most serious threat to the global environment.

When foreign pressure was brought to bear on China's environmental management during the 1980s, Beijing responded cooperatively. It established a national Environmental Protection Agency and a legal basis for environmental enforcement in 1989. The EPA, however, is a subministerial organ that is thoroughly outgunned by the industrial ministries and provinces it is supposed to supervise; the ministries and provinces have both higher bureaucratic rank and greater actual political power. The EPA's subordinate environmental protection bureaus at the provincial level and below are under the dual leadership of the EPA and local governments: the EPA provides technical guidance, and the local governments provide administrative direction.[15] Under these circumstances, environmental officials are unable to discipline the actions of the local governments.

The lack of national priority given to environmental problems is reflected in the paucity of funds devoted to them. Beijing planned to spend 0.85 percent of GNP annually on environmental protection during the Eighth Five-Year Plan (1991–95); however, during the first several years it actually provided only 0.7 percent. (Other developing countries spend an average of 1–2 percent.) Chinese EPA officials have estimated that halting further degradation would require 1.5 percent.[16] China made its commitment to the Montreal Protocol contingent on overseas aid and technology; it is eligible for aid from the UN's global environment facility estimated at $200 million, a figure Chinese and foreigners alike believe is just a drop in the bucket of what is needed to clean up past pollution and prevent future deterioration.[17] Japan, where much of China's acid rain falls, has begun devoting most of its foreign direct aid to China to the introduction of environmental technologies.

Although the PRC has begun to pay some attention to environmental problems after years of neglect, its spokespeople in international environmental forums may be laying a rhetorical foundation for future resistance to international pressures. The Chinese de-

15. Nadelson, "Ruined Earth."
16. Hendry, "Policy Reform When It Suits."
17. Nadelson, "Ruined Earth."

scribe their environmental protection policies as having "Chinese characteristics," an ominous tag usually used to signal commitment to the status quo.[18] The definition of an environmental protection policy with Chinese characteristics is one that does not impede economic growth. As Song Jian, the chairman of China's EPA, stated at the June 1992 Rio Conference on Environment and Development: "To talk about environment in isolation from economic development and technological progress means an environmental protection devoid of a material basis." Song said that China had worked out a set of environmental policies "that suit its national conditions," meaning that it had "maintained steady economic growth while averting a corresponding degradation of the environment, with even some local improvement."[19]

Labor Standards

The issue of labor is likely to be the one for which China has the most difficulty in complying with international standards. China's comparative advantage in the world economy lies mainly with its abundant labor supply. Low-wage, labor-intensive, light industry is the source of much of China's economic growth and its successful export drive, as well as a prime attraction for foreign investors. Accepting international labor standards that would effectively raise the cost of labor would be economically irrational from the perspective of China's leaders. Because the financial interests of central and local governments are directly tied to industrial profits, there would be strong domestic opposition to regulations raising labor costs. At the firm level, state firms, feeling competitive pressure from nonstate firms, are presently striving to lower their labor costs by reducing the supply of welfare goods they are expected to provide to their employees.

As yet, the only serious international pressure on China's labor practices has focused on prison labor. Americans have a moral objection to the export of products manufactured in prison facto-

18. Hendry, "Policy Reform When It Suits."
19. Song Jian,"China's Position on Environment and Development," *Beijing Review,* June 15, 1992, p. 12.

ries. American convicts also work in factories producing license plates and other items, but Chinese convicts include political prisoners whose only crime was expressing criticism of the communist regime. The United States is the only country that has threatened sanctions if the Chinese continue to export the products of convict labor. China acquiesced to the U.S. demand that it cease exporting goods produced by prisoners by signing a 1992 agreement. Enforcement of the agreement has ranged from lackadaisical to nonexistent for several reasons. The Chinese view the U.S. demand as arbitrary and unjustified; the central and local authorities who run the prisons desire the hard currency earnings from exports; and the U.S. Customs Service has assigned only one agent to monitor prison labor exports for the entire country.[20]

On the horizon are other labor issues that foreigners are likely to target, such as child labor, workplace safety, and freedom to organize unions. Labor unions have already raised these issues in other Asian countries and are beginning to do so in China. In November 1993, the Brussels-based International Textile, Garment and Leather Workers' Federation called for a boycott of toys made in China after several factory fires in Shenzhen killed dozens of workers. The union charged that Chinese companies barred and locked windows and doors to keep workers inside, and it claimed that more than 15,000 Chinese were killed in workplace accidents in 1992.[21] Even official Chinese labor unions have begun to pay attention to labor abuse in foreign-funded factories in southern China. A survey conducted by the Guangdong Labor Bureau and the Provincial Association of Trade Unions found that more than 70 percent of foreign-funded firms were violating workers' rights.[22]

American members of Congress are easily aroused by labor treatment issues; Senator Tom Harkin has introduced legislation

20. "Get Serious about Chinese Prison Labor," *New York Times,* July 21, 1993, p. A16.

21. Mark Clifford, "Social Engineers," *Far Eastern Economic Review,* April 14, 1994, p. 57.

22. Cary Huang, "Foreign Firms Reportedly Abusing Labor in Guangdong," *Hong Kong Standard,* May 6, 1994, p. 1, in FBIS, *China,* May 6, 1994, pp. 48–49.

to ban imports of goods produced by children under 15.[23] A few U.S. companies, such as Wal-Mart and Sears, Roebuck, are developing supplier codes of conduct that prohibit child labor and lay down other workplace standards.[24] At the insistence of the United States and France, GATT has agreed that social issues such as worker protection and safety standards will be on the agenda of GATT's successor organization, the World Trade Organization. China and other developing countries will be likely targets.

Difficulties of Deep Integration

In none of these three deep integration issues—intellectual property rights, environmental protection, or labor treatment— will China be able to achieve reform in the same way it achieved shallow integration, that is, through gradualism, administrative decentralization, and particularistic contracting. Imposing internationally imposed standards on recalcitrant bureaucrats will require rapid enforcement, central regulation, and uniform rules. Nothing in China's recent reform experience equips it to meet these challenges. To complicate the problem, Chinese elites reject most of the foreign criticism on these issues as protectionism disguised as moral principles.[25] From this perspective, what is surprising is how accommodating China, has been thus far in signing agreements and passing laws to conform to foreign demands regarding intellectual property rights, global environmental protection, and prison labor exports. Beneath the surface, however, lies a feeble enforcement effort and much less real progress than has been promised. Managers and officials are too caught up

23. Congressional Democrats who wanted to get President Clinton off the hook on China's MFN trading sanctions while still demonstrating their commitment to improving human rights in China have proposed a new focus on workers' rights instead of more general human rights. Thomas L. Friedman, "Democrats Push for a Compromise on Chinese Trade," *New York Times*, April 21, 1994, p. A4.

24. Clifford, "Social Engineers."

25. Some foreigners might agree with them. After all, for decades, China's huge economy was hived off from the world and its hundreds of millions of laborers kept off the international market. Absorbing China has provided both a stimulus to the world economy—as international capital rushes to China as a production site for exports and sales to the huge domestic market—and a threat to labor in some countries.

in the lucrative opportunities created by market reform and opening to be deflected by burdensome new regulatory tasks.

Foreign governments, firms, NGOs, and interest groups outside China are by no means agreed about pushing these deep integration issues on China. As noted earlier, only the United States and Western Europe can complain about persistent deficits in their trading relationships with China. In the United States, labor unions, environmental NGOs, entertainment and computer companies, and trade associations have intense interests in getting China to conform with international standards; and the U.S. Congress, which is responsive to these groups, is willing to use trade leverage to press their cause with China. But there are many other types of companies that are feverishly making money riding the Chinese boom and would oppose any new regulations that get in their way. Every year more businesses have joined the opposition to U.S. government use of MFN trade status to exert leverage on Chinese human rights practices. Most foreign investors in China, moreover, are overseas Chinese, who enjoy a comparative advantage because they can use family networks and relationships to reduce the risks created by the lack of property rights and other legal protections in the mainland economy. They like the Chinese business environment just as it is and tend to support Beijing's culturalist defense against external pressure. Other Asian governments and firms also are unsympathetic with Western (mainly U.S.) use of trade sanctions to tell other countries how to manage their societies.

Despite its communist political institutions, China was able to achieve rapid economic reform and shallow integration with the world economy. Now the vested interests of central and local officials in the new status quo, the atrophy of national administrative capacity, and the absence of domestic interests supporting harmonization will lead China to resist international efforts to integrate its economy more deeply by raising its process standards. Beijing officials will sign agreements and may even sometimes make good faith efforts to enforce them. But on the ground, Chinese economic life will continue to be only shallowly integrated with the world economy.

Appendix

Table A-1. *PRC Imports and Exports, Selected Years, 1950–93*
Billions of U.S. Dollars

Year	Total	Exports	Imports	Year	Total	Exports	Imports
1950	1.13	0.55	0.58	1980	38.14	18.12	20.02
1955	3.14	1.41	1.73	1981	44.03	22.01	22.02
1960	3.81	1.86	1.95	1982	41.61	22.32	19.29
1965	4.25	2.23	2.02	1983	43.62	22.23	21.39
1970	4.59	2.26	2.33	1984	53.55	26.14	27.41
1971	4.84	2.64	2.20	1985	69.60	27.35	42.25
1972	6.30	3.44	2.86	1986	73.85	30.94	42.90
1973	10.98	5.82	5.16	1987	82.65	39.44	43.22
1974	14.57	6.95	7.62	1988	102.79	47.52	55.28
1975	14.75	7.26	7.49	1989	111.68	52.54	59.14
1976	13.43	6.85	6.58	1990	115.44	62.09	53.35
1977	14.80	7.59	7.21	1991	135.63	71.84	63.79
1978	20.64	9.75	10.89	1992	165.61	85.00	80.61
1979	29.33	13.66	15.67	1993	195.71	91.76	103.95

Sources: State Statistical Bureau of the People's Republic of China, *China Statistical Yearbook 1993* (Beijing: China Statistical Information and Consultancy Service Center, 1993), p. 633 (data for 1950–92); General Administration of Customs People's Republic of China, ed., *China Customs Statistics* (Hong Kong: Economic Information and Agency, December 1993), p. 3 (data for 1993).

Figure A-1. *Direct Foreign Investment in the PRC, 1983–92*

Millions of U.S. dollars

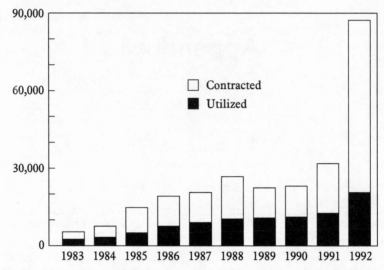

Source: State Statistical Bureau of the People's Republic of China, *China Statistical Yearbook 1993* (Beijing: China Statistical Information and Consultancy Service Center, 1993), p. 647.

Figure A-2. *PRC Imports and Exports as a Percentage of GNP, 1978–92*

Percent

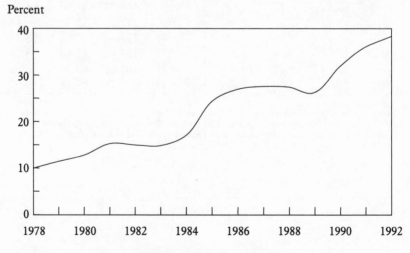

Source: State Statistical Bureau, *China Statistical Yearbook 1993*, pp. 31, 633.

Figure A-3. *Investment in Fixed Assets of State-Owned Units, by*

Percent

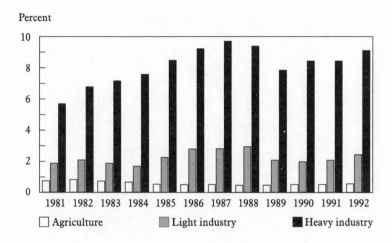

☐ Agriculture   ▨ Light industry   ■ Heavy industry

Source: State Statistical Bureau, *China Statistical Yearbook 1993,* pp. 31, 151.

Comments

Harry Harding

When Mao Zedong died in 1976, the People's Republic of China was a relatively closed and autarkic society. Although its exports had been rapidly increasing from the extremely low levels of the Cultural Revolution, they amounted only to 5 percent of China's national output, far less than those of Asia's newly industrializing economies. The system governing foreign trade—featuring state trading corporations, tight controls over foreign exchange, and a highly overvalued currency—strongly discouraged exports. China had no foreign investment and virtually no foreign debt.

Moreover, the very idea of extensive economic interaction with the rest of the world remained controversial. Foreign trade, let alone incoming foreign investment, had been portrayed by China's radical leaders as hampering China's efforts at self-reliance and therefore compromising its sovereignty. Even after the purge of the "Gang of Four," Mao's immediate successors still insisted that China would never allow the import of foreign consumer goods, foreign loans or investment, or foreign development of its natural resources.

Since launching its economic reform program in 1978, however, China has achieved a significant degree of integration with the global economy. Its trade has increased nearly tenfold, from $20 billion to almost $200 billion. Its share of global trade has more than doubled, from around 1 percent before reform to 2.5 percent today. China's absorption of foreign direct investment increased

Harry Harding is a senior fellow in the Brookings Foreign Policy Studies program.

from zero in 1978 to more than $25 billion in 1993, more than any other developing country.[1] Moreover, the forms of its engagement with the rest of the world have become more diverse and sophisticated. China has listed stocks on markets in both Hong Kong and New York; its bonds are underwritten by some of the world's most prestigious investment firms; and it is making its own direct investments overseas.

As Susan Shirk points out, these developments represent only the "shallow integration" of China and the world economy, according to the definition of the term used in this project. Like many other East Asian economies, China has been more willing to liberalize its export regime than its import regime. Tariffs, quotas, licensing requirements, and foreign exchange controls remain significant barriers to imports. China has not yet even begun to consider the key elements of "deep integration," such as coordinating its monetary, budgetary, environmental, and wage policies with those of the rest of the world.

Even so, China's achievement has been impressive. According to Nicholas Lardy, China today is arguably more fully integrated with the world economy than were Taiwan or South Korea at comparable levels of development. Given the high level of foreign direct investment in China, Lardy also suggests that China is more fully integrated with the rest of the world than Japan is today.[2]

Fragmented Authoritarianism

How did China make the passage from autarky to shallow integration so rapidly and so smoothly? Susan Shirk's essay is an informed and insightful account of an important part of the story. Drawing on her larger study of the political economy of China's domestic reform program, she discusses the complex relationship between China's central leadership and its provincial authorities and describes the bargains that had to be struck in the formulation, adoption, and implementation of China's new foreign economic policies.[3]

1. Lardy (1994, pp. 2, 30, 63).
2. Lardy (1994, pp. 110–15).
3. Shirk (1993).

From Process to Outcomes

In its focus on the bureaucratic nature of the Chinese political process, Shirk's analysis is very much in the mainstream of contemporary Western scholarship on China.[4] Ever since the Red Guards published the first accounts revealing the inner workings of the Chinese policymaking process before the Cultural Revolution, Western analysts have been interested in the degree to which different ministries and provinces have had divergent preferences on major issues and the extent to which those views influenced the formulation of policy. Since the early 1980s, foreign scholars have also been able to interview mid-level Chinese officials and knowledgeable Chinese policy analysts, thus adding much greater detail to this emerging portrait of Chinese politics. The pattern of policymaking revealed by these sources has become known as "fragmented authoritarianism." In this model, China is depicted as an essentially bureaucratic system, but one in which responsibility is divided, different agencies have different policy preferences, and top leaders must strike compromises with their subordinates in the course of policymaking and policy implementation.[5]

Thus far, most analysts have been content simply to describe the process of bargaining and consensus within the Chinese bureaucracy without fully exploring its implications for policy outcomes. In this volume, as in her earlier work, Shirk has broken important new ground. She identifies three economic policy outcomes that have resulted from fragmented authoritarianism. First, economic reform has been undertaken gradually, so as to maximize political support and minimize potential opposition at every stage.[6] Second, it has involved decentralization from the central government to the provincial authorities, rather than to markets, in order to sustain provincial backing.[7] And finally, economic reform

4. See Harding (1993); Harding (forthcoming).
5. The most important works developing this model include Lieberthal and Oksenberg (1988); Lampton (1987a); and Lieberthal and Lampton (1992).
6. Gradualism also reflects the technical complexity of economic reform and Beijing's skepticism that any foreign model or experience would be suitable to China's unique conditions.
7. This also reflects the fact that statism has had much more appeal to the present generation of Chinese leaders than has marketization. In this area, the preferences of central leaders may not have differed significantly from those of their provincial subordinates.

has involved a steady series of particularistic compromises, in which powerful provinces have been able to negotiate particular reform measures with the central government to reduce their costs and maximize their benefits. Shirk shows how several of China's most important foreign economic policy reforms—the creation of the special economic zones, foreign trade reform, and foreign exchange reform—have been shaped by China's fragmented authoritarian system.

A Decentralized System?

As Shirk points out, fragmented authoritarianism was a common characteristic of other communist systems as well as of China. Why, then, did China succeed in undertaking economic reform and opening, whereas Mikhail Gorbachev largely failed? Shirk notes correctly that the Chinese political system was far less institutionalized than its Soviet counterpart, giving China's central leadership significantly more room for maneuver. For one thing, in 1980 the Chinese bureaucratic structure had a shorter history than the Soviet *apparat:* thirty years, compared with more than sixty. Even more important, the turmoil of the Cultural Revolution had undermined whatever institutionalization had occurred, by upsetting established bureaucratic procedures, overturning the leadership at the top of the central and provincial bureaucracies, and amalgamating or disbanding large numbers of bureaucratic agencies. Although Mao's intention in launching the Cultural Revolution was to prevent the bureaucracy from sponsoring revisionism in China, the paradoxical result was to facilitate a reform program far more liberal than anything Mao could have foreseen.

Just as the bureaucracy was weaker in China than in the Soviet Union, the central leadership was simultaneously stronger. In this sense, Shirk's description of China as a "decentralized" system in the late 1970s and early 1980s may need clarification. It is true that, after the First Five-Year Plan of the early 1950s, the central *ministries* had much less power in China than in the Soviet Union. Most state-owned industries were controlled by the provincial governments, rather than by the center, and only about half of industrial output was covered by the central economic plan. Mao had been a constant advocate of administrative decentralization, and both the Great Leap Forward and the Cultural Revolution had been intended to reduce the power of the central bureaucracy over the provinces.

But Shirk is not saying that China's central *leadership* was impotent. Even after the deaths of Mao Zedong, Liu Shaoqi, and Zhou Enlai, China's three top leaders on the eve of the Cultural Revolution, the highest echelon of the Chinese Communist Party was still composed of men who had been leaders during the revolution, who thus retained the personal authority that the Andropovs and the Gorbachevs lacked in the Soviet Union. The Chinese tradition of "government by men," as opposed to "government by law," reinforced the ability of Mao's immediate successors, especially Deng Xiaoping, to assert their will over the rest of the political system.

Moreover, Deng Xiaoping used his personal authority to conduct a far more wide-ranging program of political restructuring in the early 1980s than might be inferred from a superficial reading of Shirk's analysis. Shirk's conclusion that China has "achieved economic reform without political reform" also requires explanation. To be sure, China has not made its political institutions more responsive or accountable to the popular will. There are still few competitive elections; there is no genuine multiparty system; it is still impossible to form independent nongovernmental organizations; the press is still highly constrained; and legislatures are still weak.

But in other areas there has been substantial political restructuring, deliberately intended by China's reformers to improve the prospects for economic liberalization. One such measure, which Shirk notes in passing, was the transfer of much power over economic policymaking from the Party to the government at all levels of the system. Shirk properly stresses a second aspect of political restructuring: the decentralization of authority from Beijing to the provinces. The third, and perhaps most important, measure was the turnover in central and provincial leadership engineered by the reformers between 1979 and 1985. Because of the lack of any provisions for retirement in the Maoist era, most of China's higher-level bureaucrats were superannuated. Because of the Maoist emphasis on political loyalty rather than technical competence, most of them were also poorly educated. And many were also politically vulnerable, since their very tenure in office indicated that they had either benefited from the Cultural Revolution or had made enough compromises to survive it.

The reformers' strategy was to retire these gerontocrats and replace them with officials who were younger and better educated. The reformers saw political reform not as an end in itself, as have democratic activists in Eastern Europe, but as a means of promoting the adoption and implementation of their program of economic restructuring. They used their power over broad personnel policy and specific appointments to remake China's civil service, ensuring that the new appointees would be more supportive of economic reform and, at least for a time, more responsive to the central authorities who put them in place.

At least in quantitative terms, the results were spectacular. Of the 2 million cadres still in office in the mid-1980s who had been officials in the Chinese communist movement before 1949, almost half had retired by the end of 1985, and another 700,000 had retired by the middle of 1986. Of the 333 Central Committee members in 1977, only 50 remained there by 1985. Of the thirty-seven people who held cabinet posts in 1978, only four survived until 1985. And of the twenty-nine provincial governors and first secretaries in 1979, only two remained in office in 1985. Moreover, the new appointees were significantly different in age, education, and experience from those they replaced.[8]

On balance, therefore, the Chinese political system in the early 1980s was both *more centralized* and *less institutionalized* than was its Soviet counterpart. This combination was crucial to the success of the initial stages of reform: it increased the ability of reform-minded leaders to adopt and implement a program of political restaffing and economic restructuring while simultaneously reducing the bureaucracy's ability to resist.

8. These data are drawn from Harding (1987, chap. 8).

Playing to the Provinces?

Shirk's basic thesis is that the central reformers had to ensure that their programs enjoyed sufficient support, or at least acquiescence, within the bureaucracy. Shirk portrays the reformers' basic strategy as "playing to the provinces." But because the Chinese political system in the early 1980s was not as fully decentralized as Shirk portrays it, this capsule description deserves some qualification.

It is true that provincial leaders have been an important part of what Shirk calls the "selectorate"—the Central Committee that chooses China's national elite and that must ratify national policy. China's reformers have therefore been careful to design their domestic and foreign economic policies in ways that will minimize provincial opposition and gradually build provincial support. Shirk's analysis skillfully shows how this has been done.

As an overall description of the reformers' strategy, however, "playing to the provinces" may be more alliterative than accurate. As Shirk herself points out, many of China's inland provinces (and, I would add, many northeastern coastal provinces as well) initially opposed the foreign trade and investment reforms that were granted to Guangdong, Fujian, and the special economic zones in the late 1970s and early 1980s. Only gradually did they come to realize that they would benefit from similar policies. In this sense, China's reformers played initially to only some of the provinces, while overruling or bypassing the objections of others.

Second, China's reformers have been playing to other parts of the bureaucratic establishment as well. As Shirk herself points out, they have been careful to satisfy powerful central bureaucratic interests, particularly the ministries responsible for heavy industry. They have done so by channeling a disproportionate amount of central government investment to heavy industry, by permitting the ministries of machinery and electronics to veto foreign imports in their sectors, and by providing steady subsidies to unprofitable heavy industrial enterprises. In addition, the reformers have also ensured that the military—perhaps China's most powerful single interest group—received adequate benefits from the reforms. The People's Liberation Army was promised that, once civilian modernization was well under way and the military itself had been reorganized and restaffed, it could begin to acquire more advanced weapons, including some force projection capability.

Moreover, there was another facet to the reformers' strategy to secure bureaucratic acquiescence. The reformers tried to satisfy more than just the corporate interests of key elements of the bureaucracy: the provinces' interest in growth and autonomy, the interest of heavy industry in protection and subsidy, and the military's interest in advanced weaponry. The reformers also addressed the personal interest of officials in enriching themselves and their families. Beginning in the mid-1980s, China's reformers tolerated—even welcomed—a substantial growth in official corruption. At the time, some young reform-oriented Chinese intellectuals described this as a deliberate attempt to ensure that the bureaucracy would tolerate, or even support, economic reform. In retrospect, however, the strategy has significantly undermined the legitimacy of the Party. Moreover, corruption is now so endemic that it is not clear whether the present regime can ever control it. China's reformers adopted a tactic that may have been effective in the short term but dangerously counterproductive in the longer run.

Other Factors in China's Integration

As insightful as it is, Shirk's work recounts only a portion of the story of China's integration with the global economy. A fuller rendering would deal at greater length with three additional pieces of the puzzle: Chinese leadership, Chinese society, and the international community. It is not enough to say that the Chinese bureaucracy was persuaded to accept an economic reform program, as long as that program could be shaped to meet its interests. Equally important, the central leadership was committed to China's economic integration with the rest of the world, much of Chinese society supported those efforts, and the international community was accommodating. All these elements are necessary for a comprehensive understanding of China's shallow integration into the global economy and an assessment of the prospects for China's deeper integration with the rest of the world.

China's Top Leadership

Shirk correctly assigns a greater prominence to leadership than is normally the case in studies based on models of fragmented authoritarianism. She stresses the role of the reformers in China's central leadership in launching economic reform and mobilizing the necessary political support to see it through. But her analysis does not adequately explain why they sought to do such a potentially controversial thing in the first place or how they overcame the opposition of rivals committed to more orthodox programs.

The intellectual biographies of China's reformers give a clue to their motives for reform. Some of them, like Chen Yun, had long proposed economic reforms that would allow greater room for market forces, individual ownership, and foreign economic relations. Others, like Deng Xiaoping, appear to have come fully to this realization only during the Cultural Revolution. It is likely that their commitment was intensified by their understanding that during the decade of the Cultural Revolution China had fallen behind the spectacular economic growth and technological development in Japan, South Korea, Taiwan, Hong Kong, and Singapore. In Deng's case, a strong underlying pragmatism also reinforced the conclusion that China's national power could be maximized only by undertaking economic reform.

Nor does Shirk fully describe the struggles at the top of the system, through which the proponents of China's shallow integration with the global economy managed to prevail over those who still sought a greater degree of economic autarky. In the late 1970s and early 1980s there were two such groups. The radicals surrounding the "Gang of Four" demanded that economic and cultural exchange with foreign countries be kept to a minimum, in keeping with the utopian programs of the Cultural Revolution. A second group, associated with Hua Guofeng, sought more to restore the economic system that existed in the mid-1960s, implying a significant increase in foreign trade but continued restrictions on foreign investment and cultural exchange.[9]

The reformers' appeal to provincial interests provides a partial explanation of their victory over the radicals and the restora-

9. For more on these two groups, see Harding (1987, chap. 2).

tionists. But there was much more to the story. None of the leaders of these rival factions could challenge the seniority or personal authority of Deng Xiaoping. Nor were they able to counter Deng's clever incremental strategy for gaining power: to use the backing of the army to strike decisively at the radicals, to enlarge the central leadership to make room for his own lieutenants, to dismiss some of the weaker and more controversial restorationists, and then to secure the removal of Hua Guofeng himself. Above all, both the radicals and the restorationists were tainted, to different degrees, by their association with the Cultural Revolution—the radicals as the leaders of the movement and the restorationists as opportunists who had benefited from it. Their involvement with one of the greatest disasters of modern Chinese history was the key issue that enabled the reformers to replace them as the dominant force in Chinese politics. If the reformers had not been able to do so, the prospects for economic reform in China would have been bleak indeed.

Leadership is also key to understanding the prospects for reform today. Here, the issue is twofold: first, whether the leadership will maintain a high degree of unity or will fragment over questions of personal power or policy orientation; and second, whether it will remain committed to pursuing economic reform, including China's economic integration with the rest of the world. Unfortunately, there is reason for doubt on both of these dimensions.

First of all, deeper integration and further reform will run counter to many of the leadership's policy predispositions. Political reform could loosen the Party's grip on power, producing either turmoil or the rise of a strong political opposition. Continued privatization not only runs counter to the ideological commitment to public ownership but will produce independent centers of power that could challenge the Party. Full marketization, particularly of the factors of production, raises the specter of an economy that is outside state control in a society with strong statist traditions. Permitting greater foreign participation in key sectors of the economy, through either imports or investment, threatens China's national sovereignty, another key precept for many Chinese leaders. For all these reasons, further economic and political reform may prove highly controversial within the central leadership—particularly, as I will discuss below, with regard to China's deeper integration with the global economy.

Second, it is not clear whether China's leadership will remain unified on these issues in the post-Deng era. Ever since the mid-1980s, there has been a clear division among China's reform-minded leaders between those radical reformers who were prepared to accept a higher degree of privatization, marketization, political liberalization, and integration with the world economy and the moderate reformers who were more cautious in all these areas.[10] As paramount leader, Deng Xiaoping has played a crucial role in maintaining a balance between the two groups, in essence by sacrificing leaders who sponsored political liberalization (Hu Yaobang and Zhao Ziyang) but insisting on preserving a greater degree of economic reform. In Deng's absence, the divisions between these groups could widen, resulting either in the dominance of the moderate reformers over the radical reformers or in a central government that is indecisive, immobilized, or vacillating.

Shirk's concept of "playing to the provinces" shows why such an analysis is essential to forecasting the future of reform. All of the most important issues on the economic reform agenda will prove highly controversial to the localities. Tax reform involves a redistribution of revenue flows from the provinces back to the center. Banking reform will sharply reduce the access of provincial governments to easy credit. And, by producing bankruptcy and unemployment, enterprise reform may reduce economic growth and increase political dissent in provinces with large numbers of inefficient state-owned enterprises. Further liberalization of foreign economic policy will mean greater competition for provincial enterprises. Even under the best of circumstances, Beijing will have increasing difficulty in bringing the provinces to heel. Unless the central leadership remains united and steadfast on these issues, it will be largely unable or unwilling to overcome provincial opposition, evasion, and defiance.

Chinese Society

Shirk's focus on provincial officials also slights the role of key societal forces in both launching and sustaining China's economic

10. Harding (1987, chap. 3).

reform program. Those social groups were a key source of support for China's reform-oriented leaders in the late 1970s and early 1980s. But today, societal backing for further economic reform has become more problematic. As Chinese society becomes more complex, more autonomous, and more vocal, analysis of Chinese politics can no longer focus exclusively on the central leadership and the bureaucracy.

During the early struggle between the reformers and the restorationists in the late 1970s and early 1980s, the reformers tried to mobilize the support of important sectors of Chinese society, as well as seeking the backing of members of the bureaucratic apparatus. These sectors included most notably the urban intellectuals, who had been some of the principal victims of political repression during the Maoist era and whose active participation in science, technology, education, and management would be critical to any program of economic modernization; the peasants, the most numerous group in Chinese society, whose standard of living had been most seriously compromised by Maoist economic policies and whose renewed incentive to produce could create the most rapid increase in China's economic output; and, to a lesser extent, the urban workers, who enjoyed guaranteed lifetime employment but had tightly rationed access to housing, food supplies, and other consumer goods and services.

The reformers sought this societal support even though there were neither any formal mechanisms forcing the Party to be accountable to public opinion nor any institutional devices by which societal support could be directly translated into enhanced political power. Instead, the operative mechanisms were more indirect and more subtle. One was the concern that unpopular policies and unresponsive leadership could arouse protest, possibly on a significant scale. In addition, economic modernization and faster growth required the relatively enthusiastic participation of China's labor force, particularly urban intellectuals. The fear of dissent and the need for enthusiasm—not elections or public opinion polls—were the mechanisms that made public attitudes and support relevant in an authoritarian system.

Deng's ability to play to the people was as important a factor in his triumph over Hua Guofeng and the other restorationists in the late 1970s and early 1980s as was his ability to play to the provinces. Rural output and peasant incomes rose sharply as a result of the decollectivization of agriculture. As agricultural output increased, and as private and collective services multiplied, urban workers also enjoyed a higher standard of living, although the improvements were not as dramatic in the cities as in the countryside. In particular, the "Democracy Wall" movement of late 1978 and early 1979 demonstrated that most urban workers and intellectuals supported Deng's program of repudiating the Cultural Revolution, opening China to the outside world, and launching economic reform—even if some of them also wanted more political liberalization than Deng was willing to endorse.

By the late 1980s, however, popular support for the regime began to falter as the negative consequences of reform became more apparent. There were the problems associated with a reforming economy, notably inflation, inequality, and unemployment. There was also the growth of corruption as the consequence of the reformers' miscalculation that encouraging officials to enrich themselves would be a suitable way to gain bureaucratic acquiescence to economic reform. And, perhaps most important, there was widespread dissatisfaction at the extent to which the government and Party organizations were indifferent and unresponsive to these growing popular grievances. The result was the massive anti-government protests that spread across China in the spring of 1989 and led to the bloodshed in Beijing on the night of June 3–4.

As Shirk points out, the authoritarian nature of Chinese politics prevented these grievances from derailing economic reform. The massive protests of 1989 did not force the government to reimpose controls over the economy to prevent inflation, promote equality, or protect jobs from foreign competition, as might have occurred in a country taking a more democratic path to economic liberalization.

But the complex imprint of societal attitudes on China's economic reform program is still visible. There are now powerful groups in society that are committed to reform. The beneficiaries of economic liberalization and integration with the global economy include private entrepreneurs, managers and workers in enterprises that produce for export, and intellectuals who are able to engage in cultural and academic exchange with foreign countries. While these groups may challenge particular reform policies or object to the unwanted consequences of reform, they will oppose any effort to reverse the national commitment to economic liberalization.

In addition, societal grievances have paradoxically reinforced the leadership's commitment to the broad outlines of economic reform. For a time, the Tiananmen protests prompted a renewed debate within the leadership over the desirability of continuing reform. But the prevailing view was that continued reliance on domestic markets and foreign exports was the best way to sustain high rates of economic growth, which in turn was the best way to preserve and rebuild the Party's flagging legitimacy. In particular, there was considerable fear that any attempt to restrict China's township and village enterprises, privately run enterprises, or foreign ventures would reduce growth, produce unemployment, limit exports, and thus undermine political stability.

However, societal grievances have complicated the leadership's attempts to deal with other aspects of China's economic reform agenda. Many leaders (particularly Deng Xiaoping) are concerned that slower economic growth would produce social unrest. Everyone would suffer relatively, compared with the more rapid rates of the past, and some might even suffer absolutely, as the lagging regions and sectors experience zero or even negative growth. A commitment to rapid growth, though, undermines any banking reforms that would tighten credit and any enterprise reforms that would produce bankruptcy and unemployment. The regime seems particularly reluctant to harm the interests of urban workers, who are now regarded as one of the social groups most prone to organized protest. China's central leaders may be willing to rely on the police and the army to suppress dissent, but they are also eager to avoid the economic disruptions that would produce that dissent in the first place.

The International Community

The attitude of the international community—particularly the United States as the leading developed economy—was a final impetus to China's shallow integration with the global economy in the 1980s. The world's posture toward China was generally welcoming but increasingly demanding. Governments and international financial institutions welcomed China's emergence from economic autarky and political isolation. But the business community, and increasingly key governments as well, insisted that economic reform be a condition for China's economic integration with the rest of the world.

The willingness of the West in general, and the United States in particular, to accommodate China's engagement with the international economy stands in sharp contrast to the more skeptical attitude toward the Soviet Union in the 1980s. To a degree, the enthusiasm about China was motivated by the long-standing attraction of the potentially huge Chinese market, at a time when it was difficult to foresee that China would become a major exporter of manufactured goods and thus a competitor with industries in other countries. But the main rationale was strategic: the desire (in the case of the United States) to solidify China's place in an anti-Soviet coalition, or the hope (in the case of Japan and many Asian nations) to ensure that China would play a more responsible role in the region as its economic interdependencies increased. This explains why the United States granted China most-favored-nation status so early while refusing to do so for the Soviet Union. It also explains why Japan soon made China one of the largest recipients of its official development assistance program.

The major international financial institutions also took an accommodating position toward China. As Harold K. Jacobson and Michel Oksenberg have shown, World Bank President Robert McNamara became interested in Chinese membership as early as 1973, just after Beijing had joined the United Nations, on the grounds that the World Bank could not live up to its name if the world's largest developing country were excluded. Opposition by the United States at first prevented the World Bank from acting on McNamara's instincts. But once U.S.-China relations had been normalized, the World Bank moved rapidly to encourage Chinese membership, as did the International Monetary Fund and, a few years later, the Asian Development Bank.[11]

11. Jacobson and Oksenberg (1990).

Although membership in the World Bank required that Beijing accept an unprecedented (and somewhat unwelcome) degree of transparency in its economic data, it was the private sector that placed the greatest demands on the terms of China's integration into the global economy. Importers pressed to have direct contact with the enterprises that produced goods for sale abroad, rather than working exclusively through state trading corporations. Exporters wanted greater access to the Chinese market, pushing for lower quotas, lower tariffs, and looser controls on foreign exchange. Potential foreign investors wanted the right to produce for the domestic Chinese market, as well as relief from shortages of renminbi credits, overpriced inputs, poorly trained workers, and uncertain access to raw materials distributed under the state plan.

Nor were the demands of the foreign business community restricted to matters of economic policy. Many of their requests implied the need for political reform as well. No matter what their business—import, export, or investment—foreign entrepreneurs demanded a more transparent system of regulations, the further development of commercial law, and clearer lines of authority within the bureaucracy. In addition, the foreign business community was quick to criticize any return to political orthodoxy in China. Campaigns against "bourgeois liberalization" and "spiritual pollution" in the mid-1980s were brought to an end in part because they threatened to reduce the inflow of foreign investment.

Over time, the grievances of the private business community have been sponsored by governments, particularly that of the United States. As the bilateral American trade balance with China shifted from surplus to deficit in the mid-1980s, Washington began to push Beijing for further liberalization of restrictions on trade and investment. It threatened economic sanctions, as authorized by section 301 of the Trade Act, to lower barriers to market access and to halt infringement of intellectual property rights. Conversely, it also offered China membership in the General Agreement on Tariffs and Trade (later the World Trade Organization) if it would agree to reduce tariffs, eliminate quotas and other nontariff barriers, give national treatment to foreign investors, and make its regulations more transparent. These external pressures have been major factors in promoting a central commitment to further liberalization of China's foreign economic relations and in securing provincial acquiescence for such reforms.

In short, the international community has welcomed and promoted China's shallow integration into the world economy but set the terms under which it could occur. In both Beijing and the provinces, Chinese officials have come to understand that they could not reap the rewards of international integration unless they were willing to meet the terms established by various international regimes, the norms of the international trading system, and the standards of the international business community. To be sure, they have tried to meet as few of the more inconvenient of those terms as possible, and they may fail to fulfill the commitments they assume. But without international pressure, China would undertake less wide-ranging integration than is presently the case.

The Prospects for China's Deeper Integration

Looking ahead, it will be essential to give attention to all four of these elements—leadership, bureaucracy, society, and the international community—when forecasting the prospects for China's further integration into the world economy. If these factors have generally promoted China's shallow integration with the rest of the world, they may obstruct or even prevent China's deeper integration with the world economy.

First, China's leadership is not as committed to deeper integration as it is to shallow integration. Not only does it perceive deeper integration to be a challenge to its sovereignty, but it also regards demands from the developed countries for coordinated policies on environmental protection and workers' rights as simply a disguised form of protectionism. Although younger generations of leaders may be somewhat more willing to consider policies of deeper integration, at present it is unlikely that China's leadership will invest the same amount of political capital to promote these policies as they did to promote the shallower forms of economic integration.

Similarly, parts of China's bureaucracy will be unenthusiastic about deeper integration for many of the same reasons. Deeper integration will mean greater competition from foreign firms and less insulation from foreign pressures on such issues as intellectual property rights, environmental protection, and working conditions. As Shirk points out, although reforms in these areas can be phased in gradually, these issues will be less susceptible to the particularistic bargaining with individual industries and regions that characterized Chinese economic reform in the past.

Moreover, the tendencies toward institutionalization and administrative decentralization mean that the bureaucracy, particularly in the provinces, will be better able to resist or evade central policies with which it disagrees. Increasingly, the issue in China's economic integration with the rest of the world will be the refusal of provincial authorities to fulfill any international obligations undertaken by the central government to liberalize import restrictions, protect intellectual property, control illegal exports, or terminate export subsidies. As noted above, this will be especially true if China's national leadership lacks the unity and commitment to press for further economic liberalization and international integration.

Chinese society will be divided over the merits of deeper integration into the world economy. Some intellectuals may welcome the coordination of environmental policies. Some workers may similarly applaud foreign pressure to ensure that China's policies on wages, working conditions, and safety standards comply with international norms. But there will be widespread dissatisfaction if deeper integration leads to slower growth and especially if it produces enterprise bankruptcy and unemployment. Moreover, increasing foreign intervention in the Chinese economy may promote the rise of popular nationalism, which will resist China's deeper integration with the rest of the world. The fear of social unrest, whether motivated by nationalism or by material economic interests, will be a major factor constraining both the bureaucracy and the central leadership from pursuing further economic reforms in either domestic or foreign spheres.

Finally, the international community is presently sending China much less consistent messages about deeper integration than it did about shallow integration. As noted above, major international institutions such as the World Bank and the IMF were eager to see Chinese participation in the late 1970s and early 1980s. From Beijing's perspective, however, the GATT is much less accommodating to China's membership, and there are few signs that the leading institutions that manage deeper integration, such as the OECD and the G-7, are open to Chinese participation on an equal footing.

Conversely, Beijing had little doubt in the 1980s about the terms that the rest of the world would impose on its shallow integration into the global economy: it would have to become more transparent, reduce administrative controls over the economy, reduce tariffs and nontariff barriers, and provide a more hospitable climate for foreign investment. Today, in contrast, there is no clear evidence that the rest of the world agrees on the desirability of deeper integration or on the most appropriate terms for achieving it. This opens the possibility that, rather than accepting international demands for closer integration, China will work with like-minded developing countries to deny the legitimacy of the very concept.

Taken together, these considerations all suggest that it is highly unlikely that China's deeper integration into the global economy will occur as smoothly and successfully as its more shallow integration. There may be more difficulty in persuading China to complete the unfinished agenda of shallow integration (the liberalization of import restrictions) or to accept the emerging agenda of deeper integration.

Conclusion

In short, China's institutional structure, so well described by Susan Shirk, has been a critically important factor in shaping the patterns of China's shallow integration with the global economy. One may ask whether central reformers focused so exclusively on provincial leaders when creating their initial base of bureaucratic support. But there is no denying that Shirk's analysis masterfully explains why China's opening to the outside world has proceeded gradually, why economic decentralization has granted more power to provincial governments than to the marketplace, and why reform has been characterized by so many particularistic bargains between the central and provincial authorities.

But a focus on only the bureaucracy and its interaction with the central leadership will lead to incomplete understanding of China's domestic and foreign economic reforms. One will be able to grasp the details of reforms but not why they have been attempted or abandoned in the first place.

To comprehend this larger picture, one must also examine the character and calculations of China's national leadership, the distribution of power and opinion within Chinese society, and the attitudes of the international community toward China's involvement with the global economy. Such an analysis can not only provide a fuller explanation of why China's shallow integration with the global economy has been so largely successful but can also predict that China's deeper integration with the world economy will be far more halting and troubled.

References

Bates, Robert H. 1981. *Markets and States in Tropical Africa: The Political Basis of Agricultural Policies.* University of California Press.

Brzezinski, Zbigniew K., and Samuel P. Huntington. 1964. *Political Power: USA/USSR.* Viking.

Burns, John P. Forthcoming. "Strengthening Central CCP Control of Leadership Selection: The 1990 *Nomenklatura.*" *China Quarterly.*

Byrd, William. 1987. "The Impact of the Two-Tier Plan/Market System in the Chinese Industry." *Journal of Comparative Economics* 11 (September): 295–300.

Cai Wenguo. 1992. "China's GATT Membership: Selected Legal and Political Issues." *Journal of World Trade* 26 (February): 35–61.

Chang, Parris H. 1990. *Power and Policy in China,* 3d ed. Dubuque, Iowa: Kendall/Hunt Publishing Co.

Crane, George T. 1990. *The Political Economy of China's Special Economic Zones.* Armonk, N.Y.: M. E. Sharpe.

Cumings, Bruce. 1979. "The Political Economy of Chinese Foreign Policy." *Modern China* 5 (October): 411–61.

Dernberger, Robert F. 1981. "PRC Industrial Policies: Goals and Results." University of Michigan, Department of Economics.

Frieden, Jeffrey, and Ronald Rogowski. Forthcoming. "The Impact of the International Economy on National Policies: An Analytical Overview." In *International Organization,* edited by Robert Keohane and Helen Milner. Special issue.

Frisbie, John. 1988. "Balancing Foreign Exchange." *China Business Review* 15 (March–April): 24–28.

Harding, Harry. 1981. *Organizing China: The Problem of Bureaucracy, 1949–1976.* Stanford University Press.

———. 1987. *China's Second Revolution: Reform after Mao.* Brookings.

———. 1993. "The Evolution of American Scholarship on Contemporary China." In *American Studies of Contemporary China,* edited by David L. Shambaugh, 14–40. Armonk, N.Y.: M. E. Sharpe.

111

———. 1994. "The Contemporary Study of Chinese Politics: An Introduction." *China Quarterly* 139 (September): forthcoming.

Hough, Jerry F. 1991. "Understanding Gorbachev: The Importance of Politics." *Soviet Economy* 7 (April–June): 89–109.

Jacobson, Harold K., and Michael Oksenberg. 1990. *China's Participation in the IMF, the World Bank, and GATT: Toward a Global Economic Order.* University of Michigan Press.

Koves, Andras, and Paul Marer. 1991. "Economic Liberalization in Eastern Europe and in Market Economies." In *Foreign Economic Liberalization: Transformations in Socialist and Market Economies,* edited by Andras Koves and Paul Marer, 15–36. Boulder: Westview Press.

Lampton, David M. 1987a. *Policy Implementation in Post-Mao China.* University of California Press.

———. 1987b. "Water: Challenge to a Fragmented Political System." In *Policy: Implementation in Post-Mao China,* edited by David M. Lampton, 157–89. University of California Press.

Lampton, David M., and Kenneth G. Lieberthal, eds. 1992. *Bureaucracy, Politics, and Decision Making in Post-Mao China.* University of California Press.

Lardy, Nicholas R. 1978. *Economic Growth and Distribution in China.* Cambridge University Press.

———. 1992a. "Chinese Foreign Trade." *China Quarterly,* no. 131 (September): 691–720.

———. 1992b. *Foreign Trade and Economic Reform in China, 1978–1990.* Cambridge University Press.

———. 1994. *China in the World Economy.* Washington: Institute for International Economics.

Lawler, Edward E., III. 1976. "Control Systems in Organizations." In *Handbook of Industrial and Organizational Psychology,* edited by Margin Dunette, 1247–92. Chicago: Rand McNally.

Lieberthal, Kenneth G., and Michel Oksenberg. 1988. *Policymaking in China: Leaders, Structures, and Processes.* Princeton University Press.

Mac Cormac, Susan. 1993. "Eyeing the GATT." *China Business Review* 20 (March–April): 34–38.

Massey, Joseph. 1992. "301: The Successful Resolution." *China Business Review* 19 (November–December): 9–17.

McCubbins, Matthew, and Thomas Schwartz. 1984. "Congressional Oversight Overlooked: Police Patrols vs. Fire Alarms." *American Journal of Political Science* 28 (February): 165–79.

Naughton, Barry. 1986. "Finance and Reforms in Industry." In *China's Economy Looks toward the Year 2000: Selected Papers.* U.S. Congress, Joint Economic Committee, Committee Print 86-665-P, vol. 1, 622. 99 Cong. 2 sess. Government Printing Office.

———. 1988. "The Third Front: Defense Industrialization in the Chinese Interior." *China Quarterly* 115 (September): 351–86.

———. 1989. "The Pattern and Legacy of Economic Growth in the Mao Era." In *Perspectives on Modern China: Four Anniversaries,* edited by Joyce Kallgren,

Kenneth Lieberthal, Roderick MacFarquhar, and Frederick Wakeman, 226–54. Armonk, N.Y.: M. E. Sharpe.

———. 1993. "Deng Xiaoping: The Economist." *China Quarterly* 135 (September): 491–514.

Oksenberg, Michel, and James Tong. 1991. "The Evolution of Central-Provincial Fiscal Relations in China, 1971–84: The Formal System." *China Quarterly* 1 (March): 1–32.

Panagariya, Arvind. 1991. "Unraveling the Mysteries of China's Foreign Trade Regime: A View from Jiangsu Province." WPS 801. World Bank (November).

Perkins, Dwight. 1968. "The International Impact on Chinese Central Planning." In *International Planning and Central Planning,* edited by Alan A. Brown and Egon Neuberger, 177–98. University of California Press.

———. 1991. "China's Industrial and Foreign Trade Reforms." In *Foreign Economic Liberalization: Transformations in Socialist and Market Economies,* edited by Andras Koves and Paul Marer, 269–81. Boulder: Westview Press.

Potter, Pittman B. 1988. "Seeking Special Status." *China Business Review* 15 (March–April): 36–39.

Qian Yingyi and Xu Chenggang. 1993. "The M-Form Hierarchy and China's Economic Reform." *European Economic Review* 37 (April): 541–48.

Rigby, T. H. 1964. "Crypto-Politics." *Survey* 50 (January): 183–94.

Shan Weijian. 1989. "Reforms of China's Foreign Trade System: Experiences and Prospects." *China Economic Review* 1 (1): 33–35.

Shirk, Susan L. 1984. "The Domestic Political Dimensions of China's Foreign Economic Relations." In *China and the World: Chinese Foreign Policy in the Post-Mao Era,* edited by Samuel S. Kim, 57–81. Boulder: Westview Press.

———. 1989. "The Political Economy of Chinese Industrial Reform." In *Remaking the Economic Institutions of Socialism: China and Eastern Europe,* edited by Victor Nee and David Stark, 328–69. Stanford University Press.

———. 1990. "China: The Bargaining Game." In *Technological Challenge in the Asia-Pacific Economy,* edited by Hadi Soesastro and Mari Pangestu, 158–76. Sydney: Allen and Unwin.

———. 1993. *The Political Logic of Economic Reform in China.* University of California Press.

———. Forthcoming. "Opening China to the World Economy: Communist Institutions and Foreign Economic Policy Reforms." In *International Organization,* edited by Robert Keohane and Helen Milner. Special issue.

Simone, Joseph T., Jr. 1992. "Improving Protection of Intellectual Property." *China Business Review* 19 (March–April): 9–11.

A Summary Chronology of Major Events of PRC National Economic and Social Development Planning, 1949–1985. 1987. Beijing: Hongqi Chubanshe. Cited in Dali L. Yang, "Reforms, Resources, and Regional Cleavages: The Political Economy of Coast-Interior Relations in Mainland China," *Issues and Studies,* vol. 27 (September 1987), p. 56.

Tzeng Fuh-wen. 1991. "The Political Economy of China's Coastal Development Strategy: A Preliminary Analysis." *Asian Survey* 31 (March): 270–84.

Wang, James C. F. 1992. *Contemporary Chinese Politics: An Introduction,* 4th ed. Prentice-Hall.

Wong, Christine P. W. 1986. "Ownership and Control in the Chinese Industry: The Maoist Legacy and Prospects for the 1980s." In *China's Economy Looks toward the Year 2000: Selected Papers.* U.S. Congress, Joint Economic Committee, Committee Print 86-665-P, vol. 1, 571–603. 99 Cong. 2 sess. Government Printing Office.

World Bank. 1994. *China: Foreign Trade Reform.* Washington.

Wu Jinglian and Zhao Renwei. 1987. "The Dual Pricing System in China's Industry." *Journal of Comparative Economics* 11 (September): 309–18.

Yang, Dali L. 1991a. "China Ajusts to the World Economy: The Political Economy of China's Coastal Development Strategy." *Pacific Affairs* 64 (Spring): 42–64.

———. 1991b. "Reforms, Resources, and Regional Cleavages: The Political Economy of Coast-Interior Relations in Mainland China." *Issues and Studies* 27 (September): 43–69.

Yowell, Diane. 1988. "Swap Center System to Expand." *China Business Review* 15 (September–October): 10–12.

Yu Yu-lin. 1988. "A Heated Debate on the Coastal Areas' Development Strategy." *Issues and Studies* 24 (June): 1–4.

Zheng Tuobing. 1985. "To Promote China's Foreign Trade under the Reform and Open Policy." *To Build Socialism with Chinese Characteristics,* Zhongguo Zhanwang Chubanshe. Cited in Huan Guocang, "China's Open Door Policy: 1978–1984," Ph.D. dissertation, Princeton University, 1987, p. 42.

Zhang Amei and Zou Gang. 1994. "Foreign Trade Decentralization and Its Impact on Central-Local Relations." In *Changing Central-Local Relations in China: Reform and State Capacity,* edited by Jia Hao and Lin Zhimin, 153–77. Boulder: Westview Press.

Index

115

116   Index

8, 10; Congress of, 17; delegation
by consensus in, 19–22; environmental issues and, 78; GATT and,
73; government domination by,
13–16; gradualism and, 29; institutions of, 5, 22–26; leadership competition in, 6, 17–19; nongovernmental organizations and, 77; particularistic contracting and, 32;
People's Bank of China and, 62;
Politburo, 16, 17, 18; reciprocal accountability in, 17–19, 21, 24, 31;
special economic zones and, 35.
See also Central Committee, of
Communist Party
Comparative advantage, theory of,
xvii
Computer programs, 79
Congress, U.S., 71–72, 84, 86
Convertible currency, 6, 57–58, 64–
67, 76
Coordination, xxii; escalation of,
(xietiao), 20
Copyrights, 79, 80
Corruption, 4, 33, 50–51, 98, 103
Cross-border spillovers, xvi–xix,
xxi
Cultural Revolution, 23, 93, 94, 95,
96, 99, 100, 103
Customs Service, U.S., 84

Decentralization, monitored, xxii.
See also Administrative decentralization
Deep integration, 6–7, 92; Chinese
leadership and, 100, 101; difficulties of, 85–86; environmental issues in, 4, 7, 77–78, 81–83, 85, 86,
108; intellectual property rights in,
4, 7, 77–78, 79–81, 85; labor standards in, 4, 7, 77–78, 83–85, 86,
108; prospects for, 107–09
Delegation by consensus, 19–22
Democracy Wall movement, 103
Deng Xiaoping, 6, 11, 12, 18, 21–22,
24, 25; Chinese society and, 102–

03, 104; leadership provided by,
95, 99, 100, 101; special economic
zones and, 36, 37, 39
Devaluation, 51, 56–57, 58–60, 64–65
Development zone policy, 41–42
Diminished autonomy, xviii–xix
Domestic market, opening of, 6,
67–75
Dual exchange rates, 5, 49, 51, 57–59

Economic and Trading Commissions,
47
Economic reforms, particularism of.
See Particularistic contracting
Eighth Five-Year Plan, 82
Electronics industry, 29, 56, 69–70,
74–75, 97
Environmental issues, xv–xvii, 4, 7,
77–78, 81–83, 85, 86, 108
Environmental Protection Agency
(China), 82, 83
European Community, xvi, xxi, 67
European Union, xxii–xxiii
Exchange rate convertibility. See Convertible currency
Explicit harmonization, xxii
Export certificates, 66–67
Export licenses, 47, 49
Exports, 29, 56, 57, 91, 92, 108; administrative decentralization and,
44, 48, 50, 51, 54; command economy and, 9, 11; convertible currency and, 66–67; devaluation and,
58, 59–60; foreign trade contracting and, 53; GATT and, 70, 74–
75; international community and,
106; joint ventures and, 2; labor
standards and, 83, 84; promotion
of, 68, 104; rate of increase in, 1;
special economic zones and, 38
Export subsidies, 56; administrative
decentralization and, 31; deep integration and, 108; dual exchange
rates as, 57, 59; foreign trade contracting and, 52
Externalities, xix–xxi